THE SERVILE STATE

By HILAIRE BELLOC

Page 3

SOCIALISM and the SERVILE STATE

A DEBATE BETWEEN MESSRS.
Hilaire Belloc and
J. Ramsay MacDonald, M.P.

Page 191

THE SERVILE STATE

By HILAIRE BELLOC

" . . . If we do not restore the Institution of Property we cannot escape restoring the Institution of Slavery; there is no third course."

SYNOPSIS OF THE SERVILE STATE

allowed to do the second thing by establishing servile conditions—He is forbidden to do the first—The Statistician is quite content so long as he can run and organise the poor—Both are canalised towards the Servile State and both are shepherded off their ideal Collectivist State—Meanwhile the great mass, the proletariat, upon whom the reformers are at work, though retaining the instinct of ownership, has lost any experience of it and is subject to private law much more than to the law of the Courts—This is exactly what happened in the past during the converse change from Slavery to Freedom—Private Law became stronger than Public at the beginning of the Dark Ages—The owners welcomed the changes which maintained them in ownership and yet increased the security of their revenue—To-day the non-owners will welcome whatever keeps them a wage-earning class but increases their wages and their security without insisting on the expropriation of the owners.........................page 119

An Appendix showing that the Collectivist proposal to "Buy-Out" the Capitalist in lieu of expropriating him is vain.

SECTION IX

THE SERVILE STATE HAS BEGUN:—The manifestation of the Servile State in law or proposals of law will fall into two sorts—*(a)* Laws or proposals of law compelling the proletariat to work—*(b)* Financial operations riveting the grip of capitalists more strongly upon society—As to (a), we find it ALREADY at work in measures such as the Insurance Act and proposals such as Compulsory Arbitration, the enforcement of Trades Union bargains and the erection of "Labour

INTRODUCTION

THE SUBJECT OF THIS BOOK

INTRODUCTION THE SUBJECT OF THIS BOOK

This book is written to maintain and prove the following truth: —

That our free modern society in which the means of production are owned by a few being necessarily in unstable equilibrium, it is tending to reach a condition of stable equilibrium BY THE ESTABLISHMENT OF COMPULSORY LABOUR LEGALLY ENFORCIBLE UPON THOSE WHO DO NOT OWN THE MEANS OF PRODUCTION FOR THE ADVANTAGE OF THOSE WHO DO. With this principle of compulsion applied against the non-owners there must also come a difference in their status; and in the eyes of society and of its positive law men will be divided into two sets : the first economically free and politically free, possessed of the means of production, and securely confirmed in that possession; the second economically unfree and politically unfree, but at first secured by their very lack of freedom in certain necessaries of life and in a minimum of well-being beneath which they shall not fall.

Society having reached such a condition would be released from its present internal strains and would have taken on a form which would be stable: that is, capable of being indefinitely prolonged without change. In it would be resolved the various factors of instability which increasingly disturb that form of society called *Capitalist*, and men would be satisfied to accept, and to continue in, such a settlement.

To such a stable society I shall give, for reasons

which will be described in the next section, the title of THE SERVILE STATE.

I shall not undertake to judge whether this approaching organisation of our modern society be good or evil. I shall concern myself only with showing the necessary tendency towards it which has long existed and the recent social provisions which show that it has actually begun.

This new state will be acceptable to those who desire consciously or by implication the re-establishment among us of a difference of status between possessor and non-possessor: it will be distasteful to those who regard such a distinction with ill favour or with dread.

My business will not be to enter into the discussion between these two types of modern thinkers, but to point out to each and to both that that which the one favours and the other would fly is upon them.

I shall prove my thesis in particular from the case of the industrial society of Great Britain, including that small, alien, and exceptional corner of Ireland, which suffers or enjoys industrial conditions to-day.

I shall divide the matter thus:—

(1) I shall lay down certain definitions.

(2) Next, I shall describe the institution of slavery and THE SERVILE STATE of which it is the basis, as these were in the ancient world.

I shall then:

(3) Sketch very briefly the process whereby that age-long institution of slavery was slowly dissolved during the Christian centuries, and whereby the resulting mediaeval system, based upon highly divided property in the means of production, was

(4) wrecked in certain areas of Europe as it approached completion, and had substituted for it, in practice though not in legal theory, a society based upon CAPITALISM.

(5) Next, I shall show how Capitalism was of its nature unstable, because its social realities were in conflict with all existing or possible systems of law, and because its effects in denying *sufficiency* and *security* were intolerable to men; how being thus *unstable*, it consequently presented a *problem* which demanded a solution : to wit, the establishment of some stable form of society whose law and social practice should correspond, and whose economic results, by providing *sufficiency* and *security*, should be tolerable to human nature.

(6) I shall next present the only three possible solutions:—

(*a*) Collectivism, or the placing of the means of production in the hands of the political officers of the community.

(*b*) Property, or the re-establishment of a

Distributive State in which the mass of citizens should severally own the means of production.

(*c*) Slavery, or a Servile State in which those who do not own the means of production shall be legally compelled to work for those who do, and shall receive in exchange a security of livelihood.

Now, seeing the distaste which the remains of our long Christian tradition has bred in us for directly advocating the third solution and boldly supporting the re-establishment of slavery, the first two alone are open to reformers: (*1*) a reaction towards a condition of well-divided property or the *Distributive State*; (*2*) an attempt to achieve the ideal *Collectivist State.*

It can easily be shown that this second solution appeals most naturally and easily to a society already Capitalist on account of the difficulty which such a society has to discover the energy, the will, and the vision requisite for the first solution.

(7) I shall next proceed to show how the pursuit of this ideal Collectivist State, which is bred of Capitalism leads men acting upon a Capitalist society not towards the Collectivist State nor anything like it, but to that third utterly different thing the *Servile State.*

To this eighth section I shall add an appendix showing how the attempt to achieve Collectivism gradually by public purchase is based upon an illusion.

(8) Recognising that theoretical argument of this kind, though intellectually convincing, is not sufficient to

the establishment of my thesis, I shall conclude by giving examples from modern English legislation, which examples prove that the Servile State is actually upon us.

Such is the scheme I design for this book.

SECTION ONE

DEFINITIONS

Man, like every other organism, can only live by the transformation of his environment to his own use. He must transform his environment from a condition where it is less to a condition where it is more subservient to his needs.

That special, conscious, and intelligent transformation of his environment which is peculiar to the peculiar intelligence and creative faculty of man we call the *Production of Wealth.*

Wealth is matter which has been consciously and intelligently transformed from a condition in which it is less to a condition in which it is more serviceable to a human need.

Without *Wealth* man cannot exist. The production of it is a necessity to him, and though it proceeds from the more to the less necessary, and even to those forms of production which we call luxuries, yet in any given human society there is a certain *kind* and a certain *amount* of wealth without which human life cannot be lived: as, for instance, in England to-day, certain forms of cooked and elaborately prepared food, clothing, warmth, and habitation.

Therefore, to control the production of wealth is to control human life itself. To refuse man the opportunity for the production of wealth is to refuse him the opportunity for life; and, in general, the way in which the production of wealth is by law permitted is the only way in which the citizens can legally exist. Wealth can only be produced by the application of human energy, mental and physical, to the forces of nature around us, and to the material which those forces inform.

This human energy so applicable to the material world and its forces we will call *Labour*. As for that material and those natural forces, we will call them, for the sake of shortness, by the narrow, but conventionally accepted, term *Land*.

It would seem, therefore, that all problems connected with the production of wealth, and all discussion thereupon, involve but two principal original factors, to wit, *Labour* and *Land*. But it so happens that the conscious, artificial, and intelligent action of man upon nature, corresponding to his peculiar character compared with other created beings, introduces a third factor of the utmost importance.

Man proceeds to create wealth by ingenious methods of varying and often increasing complexity, and aids himself by the construction of *implements*. These soon become in each new department of the production as truly necessary to that production as *labour* and *land*. Further, any process of production takes a certain time; during that time the producer must be fed, and clothed, and housed, and the rest of it. There must therefore be an *accumulation of wealth* created in the past, and reserved with the object of maintaining labour during its effort to produce for the future.

Whether it be the making of an instrument or tool,

or the setting aside of a store of provisions, *labour* applied to *land* for either purpose is not producing wealth for immediate consumption. It is setting aside and reserving somewhat, and that *somewhat* is always necessary in varying proportions according to the simplicity or complexity of the economic society to the production of wealth.

To such wealth reserved and set aside for the purposes of future production, and not for immediate consumption, whether it be in the form of instruments and tools, or in the form of stores for the maintenance of labour during the process of production, we give the name of *Capital*.

There are thus three factors in the production of all human wealth, which we may conventionally term *Land*, *Capital*, and *Labour*.

When we talk of the *Means of Production* we signify land and capital combined. Thus, when we say that a man is "dispossessed of the means of production," or cannot produce wealth save by the leave of another who "possesses the means of production," we mean that he is the master only of his labour and has no control, in any useful amount, over either capital, or land, or both combined.

A man politically free, that is, one who enjoys the right before the law to exercise his energies when he pleases (or not at all if he does not so please), but not possessed by legal right of control over any useful amount of the means of production, we call *proletarian*, and any considerable class composed of such men we call a *proletariat.*

Property is a term used for that arrangement in society whereby the control of land and of wealth made from land, including therefore all the means of production, is vested in some person or corporation. Thus we may say of a building, including the land upon which it stands, that it is the "property" of such and such a citizen, or family, or college, or of the State, meaning that those who "own" such property are guaranteed by the laws in the right to use it or withhold it from use. *Private property* signifies such wealth (including the means of production) as may, by the arrangements of society, be in the control of persons or corporations *other* than the political bodies of which these persons or corporations are in another aspect members. What distinguishes private property is not that the possessor thereof is less than the State, or is only a part of the State (for were that so we should talk of municipal property as private property), but rather that the owner may exercise his control over it to his own advantage, and not as a trustee for society, nor in the hierarchy of political institutions. Thus Mr. Jones is a citizen of Manchester, but he does not own his private property as a citizen of Manchester, he owns it as Mr. Jones, whereas, if the house next to his own be owned by the Manchester municipality, they own it only because they are a political body standing for the whole community of the town. Mr. Jones might move to Glasgow and still own his property in Manchester, but the municipality of Manchester can only own its property in connection with the corporate political life of the town.

An ideal society in which the means of production should be in the hands of the political officers of the community we call *Collectivist*, or more generally *Socialist*.*

A society in which private property in land and capital, that is, the ownership and therefore the control of the means of production, is confined to some number of free citizens not large enough to determine the social mass of the State, while the rest have not such property and are therefore proletarian, we call *Capitalist*; and the method by which wealth is produced in such a society can only be the application of labour, the determining mass of which must necessarily be proletarian, to land and capital, in such fashion that, of the total wealth produced, the Proletariat which labours shall only receive a portion.

The two marks, then, defining the Capitalist State are: (*1*) That the citizens thereof are politically free: i.e. can use or withhold at will their possessions or their labour, but are also (*2*) divided into capitalist and proletarian in such proportions that the State as a whole is not characterised by the institution of ownership among free citizens, but by the restriction of ownership to a section markedly less than the whole, or even to a small minority. Such a *Capitalist State* is essentially divided into two classes of free citizens, the one capitalist or owning, the other propertyless or proletarian.

---

* Save in this special sense of "Collectivist," the word "Socialist" has either no clear meaning, or is used synonymously with other older and better-known words.

My last definition concerns the Servile State itself, and since the idea is both somewhat novel and also the subject of this book, I will not only establish but expand its definition.

The definition of the Servile State is as follows:—

> "*That arrangement of society in which so considerable a number of the families and individuals are constrained by positive law to labour for the advantage of other families and individuals as to stamp the whole community with the mark of such labour we call* THE SERVILE STATE."

Note first certain negative limitations in the above which must be clearly seized if we are not to lose clear thinking in a fog of metaphor and rhetoric.

That society is not servile in which men are intelligently constrained to labour by enthusiasm, by a religious tenet, or indirectly from fear of destitution, or directly from love of gain, or from the common sense which teaches them that by their labour they may increase their wellbeing.

A clear boundary exists between the servile and the non-servile condition of labour, and the conditions upon either side of that boundary utterly differ one from another. Where there is *compulsion* applicable by *positive law* to men of a certain status, and such compulsion enforced in the last resort by the powers at the disposal of the State, there is the institution of *Slavery*; and if that institution be sufficiently expanded the whole State may be said to repose upon a servile basis, and is a Servile State. Where such formal, legal status is absent the conditions are not servile; and the difference between servitude and freedom, appreciable in a thousand details of actual life, is most glaring in this: that the free man can refuse his labour and use that refusal as an instrument wherewith to *bargain*, while the slave has no such instrument or power to bargain at all, but is dependent for his well-being upon the custom of society, backed by the regulation of such of its laws as may protect and guarantee the slave.

Next, let it be observed that the State is not servile because the mere institution of slavery is to be discovered somewhere within its confines. The State is only servile when so considerable a body of forced labour is affected by the compulsion of positive law as to give a character to the whole community.

Similarly, that State is not servile in which all citizens are liable to submit their energies to the compulsion of positive law, and must labour at the discretion of State officials. By loose metaphor and for rhetorical purposes men who dislike Collectivism (for instance) or the discipline of a regiment will talk of the "servile " conditions of such organisations. But for the purposes of strict definition and clear thinking it is essential to remember that a servile condition only exists by contrast with a free condition. The servile condition is present in society only when there is also present the free citizen for whose benefit the slave works under the compulsion of positive law.

Again, it should be noted that this word "servile" in no way connotes the worst, nor even necessarily a bad, arrangement of society, This point is so clear that it should hardly delay us; but a confusion between the rhetorical and the precise use of the word servile I have discovered to embarrass public discussion of the matter so much that I must once more emphasise what should be self-evident.

The discussion as to whether the institution of slavery be a good or a bad one, or be relatively better or worse than other alternative institutions, has nothing whatever to do with the exact definition of that institution. Thus Monarchy consists in throwing the responsibility for the direction of society upon an individual. One can imagine some Roman of the first century praising the new Imperial power, but through a muddle-headed tradition against "kings" swearing that he would never tolerate a "monarchy." Such a fellow would have been a very futile critic of public affairs under Trajan, but no more futile than a man who swears that nothing shall make him a "slave," though well prepared to accept laws that compel him to labour without his consent, under the force of public law, and upon terms dictated by others.

Many would argue that a man so compelled to labour, guaranteed against insecurity and against insufficiency of food, housing and clothing, promised subsistence for his old age, and a similar set of advantages for his posterity, would be a great deal better off than a free man lacking all these things. But the argument does not affect the definition attaching to the word servile. A devout Christian of blameless life drifting upon an ice-flow in the Arctic night, without food or any prospect of succour, is not so comfortably circumstanced as the Khedive of Egypt; but it would be folly in establishing the definition of the words "Christian" and "Mahommedan" to bring this contrast into account.

We must then, throughout this inquiry, keep strictly to the economic aspect of the case. Only when that is established and when the modern tendency to the re-establishment of slavery is clear, are we free to discuss the advantages and disadvantages of the revolution through which we are passing.

It must further be grasped that the essential mark of the Servile Institution does not depend upon the ownership of the slave by a particular master. That the institution of slavery tends to that form under the various forces composing human nature and human society is probable enough. That if or when slavery were re-established in England a particular man would in time be found the slave not of Capitalism in general but of, say, the Shell Oil Trust in particular, is a very likely development; and we know that in societies where the institution was of immemorial antiquity such direct possession of the slave by the free man or corporation of free men had come to be the rule. But my point is that such a mark is not essential to the character of slavery. As an initial phase in the institution of slavery, or even as a permanent phase marking society for an indefinite time, it is perfectly easy to conceive of a whole class rendered servile by positive law, and compelled by such law to labour for the advantage of another non-servile free class, without any direct act of possession permitted to one man over the person of another.

The final contrast thus established between slave and free might be maintained by the State guaranteeing to the *un-free*, security in their subsistence, to the *free*, security in their property and profits, rent and interest. What would mark the slave in such a society would be his belonging to that set or status which was compelled by no matter what definition to labour, and was thus cut off from the other set or status not compelled to labour, but free to labour or not as it willed.

Again, the Servile State would certainly exist even though a man, being only compelled to labour during a portion of his time, were free to bargain and even to accumulate in his "free" time. The old lawyers used to distinguish between a serf "in gross" and a serf "regardant." A serf "in gross" was one who was a serf at all times and places, and not in respect to a particular lord. A serf "regardant" was a serf only in his bondage to serve a particular lord. He was free as against other men. And one might perfectly well have slaves who were only slaves "regardant" to a particular type of employment during particular hours. But they would be slaves none the less, and if their hours were many and their class numerous, the State which they supported would be a Servile State.

Lastly, let it be remembered that the servile

condition remains as truly an institution of the State when it attaches permanently and irrevocably at any one time to a particular set of human beings as when it attaches to a particular class throughout their lives.

Thus the laws of Paganism permitted the slave to be enfranchised by his master: it further permitted children or prisoners to be sold into slavery. The Servile Institution, though perpetually changing in the elements of its composition, was still an unchanging factor in the State. Similarly, though the State should only subject to slavery those who had less than a certain income, while leaving men free by inheritance or otherwise to pass out of, and by loss to pass into, the slave class, that slave class, though fluctuating as to its composition, would still permanently exist.

Thus, if the modern industrial State shall make a law by which servile conditions shall not attach to those capable of earning more than a certain sum by their own labour, but shall attach to those who earn less than this sum; or if the modern industrial State defines manual labour in a particular fashion, renders it compulsory during a fixed time for those who undertake it, but leaves them free to turn later to other occupations if they choose, undoubtedly such distinctions, though they attach to conditions and not to individuals, establish the Servile Institution.

Some considerable number must be manual workers by definition, and while they were so defined would be slaves. Here again the composition of the Servile class would fluctuate, but the class would be permanent and large enough to stamp all society. I need not insist upon the practical effect: that such a class, once established, tends to be fixed in the great majority of those which make it up, and that the individuals entering or leaving it tend to become few compared to the whole mass.

There is one last point to be considered in this definition.

It is this:—

Since, in the nature of things, a free society must enforce a contract (a free society consisting in nothing else but the enforcement of free contracts), how far can that be called a Servile condition which is the result of contract nominally or really free? In other words, is not a contract to labour, however freely entered into, servile of its nature when enforced by the State?

For instance, I have no food or clothing, nor do I possess the means of production whereby I can produce any wealth in exchange for such. I am so circumstanced that an owner of the Means of Production will not allow me access to those Means unless I sign a contract to serve him for a week at a wage of bare subsistence. Does the State in enforcing that contract make me for that week a slave?

Obviously not. For the institution of Slavery presupposes a certain attitude of mind in the free man and in the slave, a habit of living in either, and the stamp of both those habits upon society. No such effects are produced by a contract enforceable by the length of one week. The duration of human life is such, and the prospect of posterity, that the fulfilling of such a contract in no way wounds the senses of liberty and of choice.

What of a month, a year, ten years, a lifetime? Suppose an extreme case, and a destitute man to sign a contract binding him and all his children who were minors to work for a bare subsistence until his own death, or the attainment of majority of the children, whichever event might happen latest; would the State in forcing that contract be making the man a slave?

As undoubtedly as it would not be making him a slave in the first case, it would be making him a slave in the second.

One can only say to ancient sophistical difficulties of this kind, that the sense of men establishes for itself the true limits of any object, as of freedom. What freedom is, or is not, in so far as mere measure of time is concerned (though of course much else than time enters in), human habit determines; but the enforcing of a contract of service certainly or probably leaving a choice after its expiration is consonant with freedom. The enforcement of a contract probably binding one's whole life is not consonant with freedom. One binding to service a man's natural heirs is intolerable to freedom.

Consider another converse point. A man binds himself to work for life and his children after him so far as the law may permit him to bind them in a particular society, but that not for a bare subsistence, but for so large a wage that he will be wealthy in a few years, and his posterity, when the contract is completed, wealthier still. Does the State in forcing such a contract make the fortunate employee a slave? No. For it is in the essence of slavery that subsistence or little more than subsistence should be guaranteed to the slave. Slavery exists in order that the Free should benefit by its existence, and connotes a condition in which the men subjected to it may demand secure existence, but little more.

If anyone were to draw an exact line, and to say that a life-contract enforceable by law was slavery at so many shillings a week, but ceased to be slavery after that margin, his effort would be folly. None the less, there is a standard of subsistence in any one society, the guarantee of which (or little more) under an obligation to labour by compulsion is slavery, while the guarantee of very much more is not slavery.

This verbal jugglery might be continued. It is a type of verbal difficulty apparent in every inquiry open to the professional disputant, but of no effect upon the mind of the honest inquirer whose business is not dialectic but truth.

It is always possible by establishing a cross-section in a set of definitions to pose the unanswerable difficulty of degree, but that will never affect the realities of discussion. We know, for instance, what is meant by torture when it exists in a code of laws, and when it is forbidden. No imaginary difficulties of degree between pulling a man's hair and scalping him, between warming him and burning him alive, will disturb a reformer whose business it is to expunge torture from some penal code.

In the same way we know what is and what is not compulsory labour, what is and what is not the Servile Condition. Its test is, I repeat, the withdrawal from a man of his free choice to labour or not to labour, here or there, for such and such an object; and the compelling of him by positive law to labour for the advantage of others who do not fall under the same compulsion.

Where you have that, you have *slavery*: with all the manifold, spiritual, and political results of that ancient institution.

Where you have slavery affecting a class of such considerable size as to mark and determine the character of the State, there you have the Servile State.

To sum up, then:—The SERVILE STATE is that in which we find so considerable a body of families and individuals distinguished from *free citizens* by, the mark of compulsory labour as to stamp a general character upon society, and all the chief characters, good or evil, attaching to the institution of slavery will be found permeating such a State, whether the slaves be directly and personally attached to their masters, only indirectly attached through the medium of the State, or attached in a third manner through their subservience to corporations or to particular industries. The slave so compelled to labour will be one dispossessed of the means of production, and compelled by law to labour for the advantage of all or any who are possessed thereof. And the distinguishing mark of the slave proceeds from the special action upon him of a positive law which first separates one body of men, the less-free, from another, the more-free, in the function of contract within the general body of the community.

Now, from a purely Servile conception of production and of the arrangement of society we Europeans sprang. The Immemorial past of Europe is a Servile past. During some centuries which the Church raised, permeated, and constructed, Europe was gradually released or divorced from this immemorial and fundamental conception of slavery; to that conception, to that institution, our Industrial or Capitalist society is now upon its return. We are re-establishing the slave.

Before proceeding to the proof of this, I shall, in the next few pages, digress to sketch very briefly the process whereby the old Pagan slavery was transformed into a free society some centuries ago. I shall then outline the further process whereby the new non-servile society was wrecked at the Reformation in certain areas of Europe, and particularly in England. There was gradually produced in its stead the transitory phase of society (now nearing its end) called generally *Capitalism* or the *Capitalist State.*

Such a digression, being purely historical, is not logically necessary to a consideration of our subject, but it is of great value to the reader, because the knowledge of how, in reality and in the concrete, things have moved better enables us to understand the logical process whereby they tend towards a particular goal in the future.

One could prove the tendency towards the Servile State in England to-day to a man who knew nothing of the past of Europe; but that tendency will seem to him far more reasonably probable, far more a matter of experience and less a matter of mere deduction, when he knows what our society once was, and how it changed into what we know to-day.

SECTION TWO

OUR CIVILISATION WAS ORIGINALLY SERVILE

SECTION TWO
OUR CIVILISATION WAS ORIGINALLY SERVILE

In no matter what field of the European past we make our research, we find, from two thousand years ago upwards, one fundamental institution whereupon the whole of society reposes; that fundamental institution is Slavery.

There is here no distinction between the highly civilised City-State of the Mediterranean, with its letters, its plastic art, and its code of laws, with all that makes a civilization—and this stretching back far beyond any surviving record,— there is here no distinction between that civilised body and the Northern and Western societies of the Celtic tribes, or of the little known hordes that wandered in the Germanics. *All* indifferently reposed upon slavery. It was a fundamental conception of society. It was everywhere present, nowhere disputed.

There *is* a distinction (or would appear to be) between Europeans and Asiatics in this matter. The religion and morals of the one so differed in their very origin from those of the other that every social institution was touched by the contrast—and Slavery among the rest.

But with that we need not concern ourselves. My point is that our European ancestry, those men from whom we are descended and whose blood runs with little admixture in our veins, took slavery for granted, made of it the economic pivot upon which the production of wealth should turn, and never doubted but that it was normal to all human society.

It is a matter of capital importance to seize this.

An arrangement of such a sort would not have endured without intermission (and indeed without question) for many centuries, nor have been found emerging fully grown from that vast space of unrecorded time during which barbarism and civilisation flourished side by side in Europe, had there not been something in it, good or evil, native to our blood.

There was no question in those ancient societies from which we spring of making subject races into slaves by the might of conquering races. All that is the guess-work of the universities. Not only is there no proof of it, rather all the existing proof is the other way. The Greek had a Greek slave, the Latin a Latin slave, the German a German slave, the Celt a Celtic slave. The theory that "superior races" invaded a land, either drove out the original inhabitants or reduced them to slavery, is one which has no argument either from our present knowledge of man's mind or from recorded evidence. Indeed, the most striking feature of that Servile Basis upon which Paganism reposed was the human equality recognised between master and slave. The master might kill the slave, but both were of one race and each was human to the other.

This spiritual value was not, as a further pernicious piece of guess-work would dream, a "growth" or a "progress." The doctrine of human equality was inherent in the very stuff of antiquity, as it is inherent in those societies which have not lost tradition.

We may presume that the barbarian of the North would grasp the great truth with less facility than the civilised man of the Mediterranean, because barbarism everywhere shows a retrogression in intellectual power; but the proof that the Servile Institution was a social arrangement rather than a distinction of type is patent from the coincidence everywhere of Emancipation with Slavery. Pagan Europe not only thought the existence of Slaves a natural necessity to society, but equally thought that upon giving a Slave his freedom the enfranchised man would naturally step, though perhaps after the interval of some lineage, into the ranks of free society. Great poets and great artists, statesmen and soldiers were little troubled by the memory of a servile ancestry.

On the other hand, there was a perpetual recruitment of the Servile Institution just as there was a perpetual emancipation from it, proceeding year after year; and the natural or normal method of recruitment is most clearly apparent to us in the simple and barbaric societies which the observation of contemporary civilised Pagans enables us to judge.

It was poverty that made the slave.

Prisoners of war taken in set combat afforded one mode of recruitment, and there was also the raiding of men by pirates in the outer lands and the selling of them in the slave markets of the South. But at once the cause of the recruitment and the permanent support of the institution of slavery was the indigence of the man who sold himself into slavery, *or was born into it*; for it was a rule of Pagan Slavery that the slave bred the slave, and that even if one of the parents were free the offspring was a slave.

The society of antiquity, therefore, was normally divided (as must at last be the society of any servile state) into clearly marked sections: there was upon the one hand the citizen who had a voice in the conduct of the State, who would often labour—but labour of his own free will—and who was normally possessed of property; upon the other hand, there was a mass dispossessed of the means of production and compelled by positive law to labour at command.

It is true that in the further developments of society the accumulation of private savings by a slave was tolerated and that slaves so favoured did sometimes purchase their freedom.

It is further true that in the confusion of the last generations of Paganism there arose in some of the great cities a considerable class of men who, though free, were dispossessed of the means of production. But these last never existed in a sufficient proportion to stamp the whole State of society with a character drawn from their proletarian circumstance. To the end the Pagan world remained a world of free proprietors possessed, in various degrees, of the land and of the capital whereby wealth may be produced, and applying to that land and capital for the purpose of producing wealth, *compulsory* labour.

Certain features in that original Servile State from which we all spring should be carefully noted by way of conclusion.

First, though all nowadays contrast slavery with freedom to the advantage of the latter, yet men then accepted slavery freely as an alternative to indigence.

Secondly (and this is most important for our judgment of the Servile Institution as a whole, and of the chances of its return), in all those centuries we find no organised effort, nor (what is still more significant) do we find any *complaint of conscience* against the institution which condemned the bulk of human beings to forced labour.

Slaves may be found in the literary exercises of the time bewailing their lot—and joking about it; some philosophers will complain that an ideal society should contain no slaves; others will excuse the establishment of slavery upon this plea or that, while granting that it offends the dignity of man. The greater part will argue of the State that it is necessarily Servile. But no one, slave or free, dreams of abolishing or even of changing the thing. You have no martyrs for the case of "freedom" as against "slavery." The so-called Servile wars are the resistance on the part of escaped slaves to any attempt at recapture, but they are not accompanied by an accepted affirmation that servitude is an intolerable thing; nor is that note struck at all from the unknown beginnings to the Catholic endings of the Pagan world. Slavery is irksome, undignified, woeful; but it is, to them, of the nature of things.

You may say, to be brief, that this arrangement of society was the very air which Pagan Antiquity breathed.

Its great works, its leisure and its domestic life, its humour, its reserves of power, all depend upon the fact that its society was that of the Servile State.

Men were happy in that arrangement, or, at least, as happy as men ever are.

The attempt to escape by a personal effort, whether of thrift, of adventure, or of flattery to a master, from the Servile condition had never even so much of driving power behind it as the attempt many show to-day to escape from the rank of wage-earners to those of employers. Servitude did not seem a hell into which a man would rather die than sink, or out of which at any sacrifice whatsoever a man would raise himself. It was a condition accepted by those who suffered it as much as by those who enjoyed it, and a perfectly necessary part of all that men did and thought. You find no barbarian from some free place astonished at the institution of Slavery; you find no Slave pointing to a society in which Slavery was unknown as towards a happier land. To our ancestors not only for those few centuries during which we have record of their actions, but apparently during an illimitable past, the division of society into those who must work under compulsion and those who would benefit by their labour was the very plan of the State—apart from which they could hardly think of society as existing at all.

Let all this be clearly grasped. It is fundamental to an understanding of the problem before us. Slavery is no novel experience in the history of Europe; nor is one suffering an odd dream when one talks of Slavery as acceptable to European men. Slavery was of the very stuff of Europe for thousands upon thousands of years, until Europe engaged upon that considerable moral experiment called *The Faith*, which many believe to be now accomplished and discarded, and in the failure of which it would seem that the old and primary institution of Slavery must return.

For there came upon us Europeans after all those centuries, and centuries of a settled social order which was erected upon Slavery as upon a sure foundation, the experiment called the Christian Church.

Among the by-products of this experiment, very slowly emerging from the old Pagan world, and not long completed before Christendom itself suffered a shipwreck, was the exceedingly gradual transformation of the Servile State into something other: a society of owners. And how that something other did proceed from the Pagan Servile State I will next explain.

SECTION THREE

HOW THE SERVILE INSTITUTION WAS FOR A TIME DISSOLVED

SECTION THE THIRD HOW THE SERVILE INSTITUTION WAS FOR A TIME DISSOLVED

The process by which slavery disappeared among Christian men, though very lengthy in its development (it covered close upon a thousand years), and though exceedingly complicated in its detail, may be easily and briefly grasped in its main lines.

Let it first be clearly understood that the vast revolution through which the European mind passed between the first and the fourth centuries (that revolution which is often termed the Conversion of the World to Christianity, but which should for purposes of historical accuracy be called the Growth of the Church) included no attack upon the Servile Institution.

No dogma of the Church pronounced Slavery to be immoral, or the sale and purchase of men to be a sin, or the imposition of compulsory labour upon a Christian to be a contravention of any human right.

The emancipation of Slaves was indeed regarded as a good work by the Faithful: but so was it regarded by the Pagan. It was, on the face of it, a service rendered to one's fellowmen. The sale of Christians to Pagan masters was abhorrent to the later empire of the Barbarian Invasions, not because slavery in itself was condemned, but because it was a sort of treason to civilisation to force men away from Civilisation to Barbarism. In general you will discover no pronouncement against slavery as an institution, nor any moral definition attacking it, throughout all those early Christian centuries during which it none the less effectively disappears.

The form of its disappearance is well worth noting. It begins with the establishment as the fundamental unit of production in Western Europe of those great landed estates, commonly lying in the hands of a single proprietor, and generally known as VILLÆ.

There were, of course, many other forms of human agglomeration: small peasant farms owned in absolute proprietorship by their petty masters; groups of free men associated in what was called a *Vicus*; manufactories in which groups of slaves were industrially organised to the profit of their master; and, governing the regions around them, the scheme of Roman towns.

But of all these the *Villa* was the dominating type; and as society passed from the high civilisation of the first four centuries into the simplicity of the Dark Ages, the *Villa*, the unit of agricultural production, became more and more the model of all society.

Now the *Villa* began as a considerable extent of land, containing, like a modern English estate, pasture, arable, water, wood and heath, or waste land. It was owned by a *dominus* or *lord* in absolute proprietorship, to sell, or leave by will, to do with it whatsoever he chose. It was cultivated for him by *Slaves* to whom he owed nothing in return, and whom it was simply his interest to keep alive and to continue breeding in order that they might perpetuate his wealth.

I concentrate particularly upon these Slaves, the

great majority of the human beings inhabiting the land, because, although there arose in the Dark Ages, when the Roman Empire was passing into the society of the Middle Ages, other social elements within the Villa—the Freed men who owed the lord a modified service, and even occasionally independent citizens present through a contract terminable and freely entered into—yet it is the *Slave* who is the mark of all that society.

At its origin, then, the Roman *Villa* was a piece of absolute property, the production of wealth upon which was due to the application of slave labour to the natural resources of the place; and that slave labour was as much the property of the lord as was the land itself.

The first modification which this arrangement showed in the new society which accompanied the growth and establishment of the Church in the Roman world, was a sort of customary rule which modified the old arbitrary position of the Slave.

The Slave was still a Slave, but it was both more convenient in the decay of communications and public power, and more consonant with the social spirit of the time to make sure of that Slave's produce by asking him for no more than certain customary dues. The Slave and his descendants became more or less rooted to one spot. Some were still bought and sold, but in decreasing numbers. As the generations passed a larger and a larger proportion lived where and as their fathers had lived, and the produce which they raised was fixed more and more at a certain amount, which the lord was content to receive and ask no more. The arrangement was made workable by leaving to the Slave all the remaining produce of his own labour. There was a sort of implied bargain here, in the absence of public powers and in the decline of the old highly centralised and vigorous system which could always guarantee to the master the full product of the Slave's effort. The bargain implied was, that if the Slave Community of the *Villa* would produce for the benefit of its Lord not less than a certain customary amount of goods from the soil of the *Villa*, the Lord could count on their always exercising that effort by leaving to them all the surplus, which they could increase, if they willed, indefinitely.

By the ninth century, when this process had been gradually at work for a matter of some three hundred years, one fixed form of productive unit began to be apparent throughout Western Christendom.

The old absolutely owned estate had come to be divided into three portions. One of these was pasture and arable land, reserved privately to the lord, and called *domain*: that is, lord's land. Another was in the occupation, and already almost in the possession (practically, though not legally), of those who had once been Slaves. A third was common land over which both the Lord and the Slave exercised each their various rights, which rights were minutely remembered and held sacred by custom. For instance, in a certain village, if there was beech pasture for three hundred swine, the lord might put in but fifty: two hundred and fifty were the rights of the "village."

Upon the first of these portions, Domain, wealth

was produced by the obedience of the Slave for certain fixed hours of labour. He must come so many days a week, or upon such and such occasions (all fixed and customary), to till the land of the Domain for his Lord, and *all* the produce of this must be handed over to the Lord though, of course, a daily wage in kind was allowed, for the labourer must live.

Upon the second portion, "Land in Villenage," which was nearly always the most of the arable and pasture land of the *Villa*, the Slaves worked by rules and customs which they gradually came to elaborate for themselves. They worked under an officer of their own, sometimes nominated, sometimes elected: nearly always, in practice, a man suitable to them and more or less of their choice; though this co-operative work upon the old Slave-ground was controlled by the general customs of the village, common to lord and slave alike, and the principal officer over both kinds of land was the Lord's Steward.

Of the wealth so produced by the Slaves, a certain fixed portion (estimated originally in kind) was payable to the Lord's Bailiff, and became the property of the Lord.

Finally, on the third division of the land, the "Waste," the "Wood," the "Heath," and certain common pastures, wealth was produced as elsewhere by the labour of those who had once been the Slaves, but divided in customary proportions between them and their master. Thus, such and such a water meadow would have grazing for so many oxen; the number was rigidly defined, and of that number so many would be the Lord's and so many the Villagers'.

During the eighth, ninth and tenth centuries this system crystallised and became so natural in men's eyes that the original servile character of the working folk upon the *Villa* was forgotten.

The documents of the time are rare. These three centuries are the crucible of Europe, and record is drowned and burnt in them. Our study of their social conditions, especially in the latter part, are matter rather of inference than of direct evidence. But the sale and purchase of men, already exceptional at the beginning of this period. is almost unknown before the end of it. Apart from domestic slaves within the household, slavery in the old sense which Pagan antiquity gave that institution had been transformed out of all knowledge, and when, with the eleventh century, the true Middle Ages begin to spring from the soil of the Dark Ages, and a new civilisation to arise, though the old word *servus* (the Latin for a slave) is still used for the man who works the soil, his status in the now increasing number of documents which we can consult is wholly changed; we can certainly no longer translate the word by the English word slave; we are compelled to translate it by a new word with very different connotations : the word *serf*.

The Serf of the early Middle Ages, of the eleventh and early twelfth centuries, of the Crusades and the Norman Conquest, is already nearly a peasant. He is indeed bound in legal theory to the soil upon which he was born. In social practice, all that is required of him is that his family should till its quota of servile land, and that the dues to the lord shall not fail from absence of labour. That duty fulfilled, it is easy and common for members of the serf-class to enter the professions and the Church, or to go wild; to become men practically free in the growing industries of the towns. With every passing generation the ancient servile conception of the labourer's status grows more and more dim, and the Courts and the practice of society treat him more and more as a man strictly bound to certain dues and to certain periodical labour within his industrial unit, but in all other respects free.

As the civilisation of the Middle Ages develops, as wealth increases and the arts progressively flourish, this character of freedom becomes more marked. In spite of attempts in time of scarcity (as after a plague) to insist upon the old rights to compulsory labour, the habit of commuting these rights for money-payments and dues has grown too strong to be resisted.

If at the end of the fourteenth century, let us say, or at the beginning of the fifteenth, you had visited some Squire upon his estate in France or in England, he would have told you of the whole of it, "These are my lands." But the peasant (as he now was) would have said also of his holding, "This is my land." He could not be evicted from it. The dues which he was customarily bound to pay were but a fraction of its total produce. He could not always sell it, but it was always inheritable from father to son; and, in general, at the close of this long process of a thousand years the Slave had become a free man for all the ordinary purposes of society. He bought and sold. He saved as he willed, he invested, he built, he drained at his discretion, and if he improved the land it was to his own profit.

Meanwhile, side by side with this emancipation of mankind in the direct line of descent from the old chattel slaves of the Roman *villa* went, in the Middle Ages, a crowd of institutions which all similarly made for a distribution of property, and for the destruction of even the fossil remnants of a then forgotten Servile State. Thus industry of every kind in the towns, in transport, in crafts, and in commerce, was organised in the form of *Guilds*. And a Guild was a society partly co-operative, but in the main composed of private owners of capital whose corporation was self-governing, and was designed to check competition between its members: to prevent the growth of one at the expense of the other. Above all, most jealously did the Guild safeguard the division of property, so that there should be formed within its ranks no proletariat upon the one side, and no monopolising capitalist upon the other.

There was a period of apprenticeship at a man's entry into a Guild, during which he worked for a master; but in time he became a master in his turn. The existence of such corporations as the normal units of industrial production, of commercial effort, and of the means of transport, is proof enough of what the social spirit was which had also enfranchised the labourer upon the land. And while such institutions flourished side by side with the no longer servile village communities, freehold or absolute possession of the soil, as distinguished from the tenure of the serf under the lord, also increased.

These three forms under which labour was exercised—the serf, secure in his position, and burdened only with regular dues, which were but a fraction of his produce; the freeholder, a man independent save for money dues, which were more of a tax than a rent; the Guild, in which well-divided capital worked co-operatively for craft production, for transport and for commerce—all three between them were making for a society which should be based upon the principle of property. All, or most,—the normal family—should own. And on ownership the freedom of the State should repose.

The State, as the minds of men envisaged it at the close of this process, was an agglomeration of families of varying wealth, but by far the greater number owners of the means of production. It was an agglomeration in which the stability of this *distributive* system (as I have called it) was guaranteed by the existence of co-operative bodies, binding men of the same craft or of the same village together; guaranteeing the small proprietor against loss of his economic independence, while at the same time it guaranteed society against the growth of a proletariat. If liberty of purchase and of sale, of mortgage and of inheritance was restricted, it was restricted with the social object of preventing the growth of an economic oligarchy which could exploit the rest of the community. The restraints upon liberty were restraints designed for the preservation of liberty; and every action of Mediaeval Society, from the flower of the Middle Ages to the approach of their catastrophe, was directed towards the establishment of a State in which men should be economically free through the possession of capital and of land.

Save here and there in legal formulae, or in rare patches isolated and eccentric, the Servile Institution had totally disappeared; nor must it be imagined that anything in the nature of Collectivism had replaced it. There was common land, but it was common land jealously guarded by men who were also personal proprietors of other land. Common property in the village was but one of the forms of property, and was used rather as the fly-wheel to preserve the regularity of the co-operative machine than as a type of holding in any way peculiarly sacred. The Guilds had property in common, but that property was the property necessary to their co-operative life, their Halls, their Funds for Relief, their Religious Endowments. As for the instruments of their trades, those instruments were owned by the individual members, not by the guild, save where they were of so expensive a kind as to necessitate a corporate control.

Such was the transformation which had come over European society in the course of ten Christian centuries. Slavery had gone, and in its place had come that establishment of free possession which seemed so normal to men, and so consonant to a happy human life. No particular name was then found for it. To-day, and now that it has disappeared, we must construct an awkward one, and say that the Middle Ages had instinctively conceived and brought into existence the DISTRIBUTIVE STATE.

That excellent consummation of human society passed, as we know, and was in certain Provinces of Europe, but more particularly in Britain, destroyed.

For a society in which the determinant mass of families were owners of capital and of land; for one in which production was regulated by self-governing corporations of small owners; and for one in which the misery and insecurity of a proletariat was unknown, there came to be substituted the dreadful moral anarchy against which all moral effort is now turned, and which goes by the name of *Capitalism*.

How did such a catastrophe come about? Why was it permitted, and upon what historical process did the evil batten? What turned an England economically free into the England which we know to-day, of which at least one-third is indigent, of which nineteen-twentieths are dispossessed of capital and of land, and of which the whole industry and national life is controlled upon its economic side by a few chance directors of millions, a few masters of unsocial and irresponsible monopolies ?

The answer most usually given to this fundamental question in our history, and the one most readily accepted, is that this misfortune came about through a material process known as the *Industrial Revolution*. The use of expensive machinery, the concentration of industry and of its implements are imagined to have enslaved, in some blind way, apart from the human will, the action of English mankind.

The explanation is wholly false. No such material cause determined the degradation from which we suffer.

It was the deliberate action of men, evil will in a few and apathy of will among the many, which produced a catastrophe as human in its causes and inception as in its vile effect.

Capitalism was not the growth of the industrial movement, nor of chance material discoveries. A little acquaintance with history and a little straightforwardness in the teaching of it would be enough to prove that.

The Industrial System was a growth proceeding from Capitalism, not its cause. Capitalism was here in England before the Industrial System came into being;—before the use of coal and of the new expensive machinery, and of the concentration of the implements of production in the great towns. Had Capitalism not been present before the Industrial Revolution, that revolution might have proved as beneficent to Englishmen as it has proved maleficent. But Capitalism—that is, the ownership by a few of the springs of life—was present long before the great discoveries came. It warped the effect of these discoveries and new inventions, and it turned them from a good into an evil thing. It was not machinery that lost us our freedom; it was the loss of a free mind.

SECTION FOUR

HOW THE DISTRIBUTIVE STATE FAILED

SECTION THE FOURTH
HOW THE DISTRIBUTIVE STATE FAILED

With the close of the middle ages the societies of Western Christendom and England among the rest were economically free.

Property was an institution native to the State and enjoyed by the great mass of its citizens. Co-operative institutions, voluntary regulations of labour, restricted the completely independent use of property by its owners only in order to keep that institution intact and to prevent the absorption of small property by great.

This excellent state of affairs which we had reached after many centuries of Christian development, and in which the old institution of slavery had been finally eliminated from Christendom, did not everywhere survive. In England in particular it was ruined. The seeds of the disaster were sown in the sixteenth century. Its first apparent effects came to light in the seventeenth. During the eighteenth century England came to be finally, though insecurely, established upon a proletarian basis, that is, it had already become a society of rich men possessed of the means of production on the one hand, and a majority dispossessed of those means upon the other. With the nineteenth century the evil plant had come to its maturity, and England had become before the close of that period a purely Capitalist State, the type and model of Capitalism for the whole world: with the means of production tightly held by a very small group of citizens, and the whole determining mass of the nation dispossessed of capital and land, and dispossessed, therefore, in all cases of security, and in many of sufficiency as well. The mass of Englishmen, still possessed of political, lacked more and more the elements of economic, freedom, and were in a worse posture than free citizens have ever found themselves before in the history of Europe.

By what steps did so enormous a catastrophe fall upon us?

The first step in the process consisted in the mishandling of a great economic revolution which marked the sixteenth century. The lands and the accumulated wealth of the monasteries were taken out of the hands of their old possessors with the intention of vesting them in the Crown but they passed, as a fact, not into the hands of the Crown, but into the hands of an already wealthy section of the community who, after the change was complete, became in the succeeding hundred years the governing power of England.

This is what happened:—

The England of the early sixteenth century, the England over which Henry VIII inherited his powerful Crown in youth, though it was an England in which the great mass of men owned the land they tilled and the houses in which they dwelt, and the implements with which they worked, was yet an England in which these goods, though widely distributed, were distributed unequally.

Then, as now, the soil and its fixtures were the basis

of all wealth, but the proportion between the value of the soil and its fixtures and the value of other means of production (implements, stores of clothing and of subsistence, etc.) was different from what it is now. The land and the fixtures upon it formed a very much larger fraction of the totality of the means of production than they do to-day. They represent to-day not one-half the total means of production of this country, and though they are the necessary foundation for all wealth production, yet our great machines, our stores of food and clothing, our coal and oil, our ships and the rest of it, come to more than the true value of the land and of the fixtures upon the land: they come to more than the arable soil and the pasture, the constructional value of the houses, wharves and docks, and so forth. In the early sixteenth century the land and the fixtures upon it came, upon the contrary, to very much more than all other forms of wealth combined.

Now this form of wealth was here, more than in any other Western European country, already in the hands of a wealthy land-owning class at the end of the Middle Ages.

It is impossible to give exact statistics, because none were gathered, and we can only make general statements based upon inference and research. But, roughly speaking, we may say that of the total value of the land and its fixtures, probably rather more than a quarter, though less than a third, was in the hands of this wealthy class.

The England of that day was mainly agricultural,

and consisted of more than four, but less than six million people, and in every agricultural community you would have the Lord, as he was legally called (the squire, as he was already conversationally termed), in possession of more demesne land than in any other country. On the average you found him, I say, owning in this absolute fashion rather more than a quarter, perhaps a third of the land of the village: in the towns the distribution was more even. Sometimes it was a private individual who was in this position, sometimes a corporation, but in every village you would have found this demesne land absolutely owned by the political head of the village, occupying a considerable proportion of its acreage. The rest, though distributed as property among the less fortunate of the population, and carrying with it houses and implements from which they could not be dispossessed, paid certain dues to the Lord, and, what was more, the Lord exercised local justice. This class of wealthy land-owners had been also for now one hundred years the Justices upon whom local administration depended.

There was no reason why this state of affairs should not gradually have led to the rise of the Peasant and the decay of the Lord. That is what happened in France, and it might perfectly well have happened here. A peasantry eager to purchase might have gradually extended their holdings at the expense of the demesne land, and to the distribution of property, which was already fairly complete, there might have been added another excellent element, namely, the more equal possession of that property. But any such process of gradual buying by the small man from the great, such as would seem natural to the temper of us European people, and such as has since taken place nearly everywhere in countries which were left free to act upon their popular instincts, was interrupted in this country by an artificial revolution of the most violent kind. This artificial revolution consisted in the seizing of the monastic lands by the Crown.

It is important to grasp clearly the nature of this operation, for the whole economic future of England was to flow from it.

Of the *demesne* lands, and the power of local administration which they carried with them (a very important feature, as we shall see later), rather more than a quarter were in the hands of the Church; the Church was therefore the "Lord" of something over 25 per cent, say 28 per cent, or perhaps nearly 30 per cent, of English agricultural communities, and the overseers of a like proportion of all English agricultural produce. The Church was further the absolute owner in practice of something like 30 per cent, of the demesne land in the villages, and the receiver of something like 30 per cent, of the customary dues, etc., paid by the smaller owners to the greater. All this economic power lay until 1535 in the hands of Cathedral Chapters, communities of monks and nuns, educational establishments conducted by the clergy, and so forth.

When the Monastic lands were confiscated by Henry VIII., not the whole of this vast economic influence was suddenly extinguished. The secular clergy remained endowed, and most of the educational establishments, though looted, retained some revenue; but though the whole 30 per cent did not suffer confiscation, something well over 20 per cent, did, and the revolution effected by this vast operation was by far the most complete, the most sudden, and the most momentous of any that has taken place in the economic history of any European people.

It was at first *intended* to retain this great mass of the means of production in the hands of the Crown: that must be clearly remembered by any student of the fortunes of England, and by all who marvel at the contrast between the old England and the new.

Had that intention been firmly maintained, the English State and its government would have been the most powerful in Europe.

The Executive (which in those days meant the *King*) would have had a greater opportunity for crushing the resistance of the wealthy, for backing its political power with economic power, and for ordering the social life of its subjects than any other executive in Christendom.

Had Henry VIII and his successors kept the land thus confiscated, the power of the French Monarchy, at which we are astonished, would have been nothing to the power of the English.

The King of England would have had in his own hands an instrument of control of the most absolute sort. He would presumably have used it, as a strong central government always does, for the weakening of the wealthier classes, and to the indirect advantage of the mass of the people. At any rate, it would have been a very different England indeed from the England we know, if the King had held fast to his own after the dissolution of the monasteries.

Now it is precisely here that the capital point in this great revolution appears. *The King failed to keep the lands he had seized.* That class of large landowners which already existed and controlled, as I have said, anything from a quarter to a third of the agricultural values of England, were too strong for the monarchy. They insisted upon land being granted to themselves, sometimes freely, sometimes for ridiculously small sums, and they were strong enough in Parliament, and through the local administrative power they had, to see that their demands were satisfied. Nothing that the Crown let go ever went back to the Crown, and year after year more and more of what had once been the monastic land became the absolute possession of the large land-owners.

Observe the effect of this. All over England men who already held in virtually absolute property from one-quarter to one-third of the soil and the ploughs and the barns of a village, became possessed in a very few years of a further great section of the means of production, which turned the scale wholly in their favour. They added to that third a new and extra fifth. They became at a blow the owners of *half* the land! In many centres of capital importance they had come to own more than half the land. They were in many districts not only the unquestioned superiors, but the economic masters of the rest of the community. They could buy to the greatest advantage. They were strictly *competitive*, getting every shilling of due and of rent where the old clerical landlords had been *customary*—leaving much to the tenant. They began to fill the universities, the judiciary. The Crown less and less decided between great and small. More and more the great could decide in their own favour. They soon possessed by these operations the bulk of the means of production, and they immediately began the process of eating up the small independent men and gradually forming those great estates which, in the course of a few generations, became identical with the village itself. All over England you may notice that the great squires' houses date from this revolution or after it. The manorial house, the house of the local great man as it was in the Middle Ages, survives here and there to show of what immense effect this revolution was. The low-timbered place with its steadings and outbuildings, only a larger farmhouse among the other farmhouses, is turned after the Reformation and thenceforward into a palace. Save where great castles (which were only held of the Crown and not owned) made an exception, the pre-Reformation gentry lived as men richer than, but not the masters of, other farmers around them. *After* the Reformation there began to arise all over England those great "country houses" which rapidly became the typical centres of English agricultural life.

The process was in full swing before Henry died. Unfortunately for England, he left as his heir a sickly child, during the six years of whose reign, from 1547 to 1553, the loot went on at an appalling rate. When he died and Mary came to the throne it was nearly completed. A mass of new families had arisen, wealthy out of all proportion to anything which the older England had known, and bound by a common interest to the older families which had joined in the grab. Every single man who sat in Parliament for a country required his price for voting the dissolution of the monasteries; every single man received it. A list of the members of the Dissolution Parliament is enough to prove this, and, apart from their power in Parliament, this class had a hundred other ways of insisting on their will. The Howards (already of some lineage), the Cavendishes, the Cecils, the Russels, and fifty other new families thus rose upon the ruins of religion; and the process went steadily on until, about one hundred years after its inception, the whole face of England was changed.

In the place of a powerful Crown disposing of revenues far greater than that of any subject, you had a Crown at its wit's end for money, and dominated by subjects some of whom were its equals in wealth, and who could, especially through the action of Parliament (which they now controlled), do much what they willed with Government.

In other words, by the first third of the seventeenth century, by 1630-40, the economic revolution was finally accomplished, and the new economic reality thrusting itself upon the old traditions of England was a powerful oligarchy of large owners overshadowing an impoverished and dwindled monarchy.

Other causes had contributed to this deplorable result. The change in the value of money had hit the

Crown very hard;* the peculiar history of the Tudor family, their violent passions, their lack of resolution and of any continuous policy, to some extent the character of Charles I himself, and many another subsidiary cause may be quoted. But the great main fact upon which the whole thing is dependent is the fact that the Monastic Lands, at least a fifth of the wealth of the country, had been transferred to the great land-owners, and that this transference had tipped the scale over entirely in their favour as against the peasantry.

The diminished and impoverished Crown could no longer stand. It fought against the new wealth, the struggle of the Civil Wars; it was utterly defeated; and when a final settlement was arrived at in 1660, you have all the realities of power in the hands of a small powerful class of wealthy men, the King still surrounded by the forms and traditions of his old power, but in practice a salaried puppet. And in that economic world which underlies all political appearances, the great dominating note was that a few wealthy families had got hold of the bulk of the means of production in England, while the same families exercised all local administrative power and were moreover the Judges, the Higher Education, the Church, and the generals. They quite overshadowed what was left of central government in this country.

---

* The purchasing power of money fell during this century to about a third of its original standard. 3 (say) would purchase under Charles I the necessities which 1 would have purchased under Henry VIII. Nearly all the receipts of the Crown were customary. Most of its expenses were competitive. It continued to get but 1 where it was gradually compelled to pay out 3.

Take, as a starting-point for what followed, the date 1700. By that time more than half of the English were dispossessed of capital and of land. Not one man in two, even if you reckon the very small owners, inhabited a house of which he was the secure possessor, or tilled land from which he could not be turned off.

Such a proportion may seem to us to-day a wonderfully free arrangement, and certainly if nearly one-half of our population were possessed of the means of production, we should be in a very different situation from that in which we find ourselves. But the point to seize is that, though the bad business was very far from completion in or about the year 1700, yet by that date England had already become CAPITALIST. She had already permitted a vast section of her population to become *proletarian*, and it is this and *not* the so-called "Industrial Revolution," a later thing, which accounts for the terrible social condition in which we find ourselves to-day.

How true this is what I still have to say in this section will prove.

In an England thus already cursed with a very large proletariat class, and in an England already directed by a dominating Capitalist class, possessing the means of production, there came a great industrial development.

Had that industrial development come upon a people economically free, it would have taken a co-operative form. Coming as it did upon a people which had already largely lost its economic freedom, it took at its very origin a *Capitalist* form, and this form it has retained, expanded, and perfected throughout two hundred years.

It was in England that the Industrial System arose. It was in England that all its traditions and habits were formed; and because the England in which it arose was already a Capitalist England, modern Industrialism, wherever you see it at work to-day, having spread from England, has proceeded upon the Capitalist model.

It was in 1705 that the first practical steam-engine, Newcomen's, was set to work. The life of a man elapsed before this invention was made, by Watt's introduction of the condenser, into the great instrument of production which has transformed our industry— but in those sixty years all the origins of the Industrial System are to be discovered. It was just before Watt's patent that Hargreaves' spinning-jenny appeared. Thirty years earlier, Abraham Darby of Colebrook Dale, at the end of a long series of experiments which had covered more than a century, smelted iron-ore successfully with coke. Not twenty years later, King introduced the flying shuttle, the first great improvement in the hand-loom; and in general the period covered by such a life as that of Dr. Johnson, born just after Newcomen's engine was first set working, and dying seventy-four years afterwards, when the Industrial System was in full blast, covers that great transformation of England. A man who, as a child, could remember the last years of Queen Anne, and who lived to the eve of the French Revolution, saw passing before his eyes the change which transformed English society and has led it to the expansion and peril in which we see it to-day.

What was the characteristic mark of that half-century and more? Why did the new inventions give us the form of society now known and hated under the name of Industrial? Why did the vast increase in the powers of production, in population and in accumulation of wealth, turn the mass of Englishmen into a poverty-stricken proletariat, cut off the rich from the rest of the nation, and develop to the full all the evils which we associate with the Capitalist State?

To that question an answer almost as universal as it is unintelligent has been given. That answer is not only unintelligent but false, and it will be my business here to show how false it is. The answer so provided in innumerable text-books, and taken almost as a commonplace in our universities, is that the new methods of production the new machinery, the new implements fatally and of themselves developed a Capitalist State in which a few should own the means of production and the mass should be proletariat. The new instruments, it is pointed out, were on so vastly greater a scale than the old, and were so much more expensive, that the small man could not afford them; while the rich man, who could afford them, ate up by his competition, and reduced from the position of a small owner to that of a wage-earner, his insufficiently equipped competitor who still attempted to struggle on with the older and cheaper tools. To this (we are told) the advantages of concentration were added in favour of the large owner against the small. Not only were the new instruments expensive almost in proportion to their efficiency, but, especially after the introduction of steam, they were efficient in proportion to their concentration in few places and under the direction of a few men. Under the effect of such false arguments as these we have been taught to believe that the horrors of the Industrial System were a blind and necessary product of material and impersonal forces, and that wherever the steam engine, the power loom, the blast furnace and the rest were introduced, there fatally would soon appear a little group of owners exploiting a vast majority of the dispossessed.

It is astonishing that a statement so unhistorical should have gained so general a credence. Indeed, were the main truths of English history taught in our schools and universities to-day, were educated men familiar with the determining and major facts of the national past, such follies could never have taken root. The vast growth of the proletariat, the concentration of ownership into the hands of a few owners, and the exploitation by those owners of the mass of the community, had no fatal or necessary connection with the discovery of new and perpetually improving methods of production. The evil proceeded indirect historical sequence, proceeded patently and demonstrably, from the fact that England, the seed-plot of the Industrial System, was *already* captured by a wealthy oligarchy *before* the series of great discoveries began.

Consider in what way the Industrial System developed upon Capitalist lines. Why were a few rich men put with such ease into possession of the new methods? Why was it normal and natural in their eyes and in that of con temporary society that those who produced the new wealth with the new machinery should be proletarian and dispossessed? Simply because the England upon which the new discoveries had come was *already* an England owned as to its soil and accumulations of wealth by a small minority: it was *already* an England in which perhaps half of the whole population was proletarian, and a medium for exploitation ready to hand.

When any one of the new industries was launched it had to be *capitalised*; that is, accumulated wealth from some source or other had to be found which would support labour in the process of production until that process should be complete. Someone must find the corn and the meat and the housing and the clothing by which should be supported, between the extraction of the raw material and the moment when the consumption of the finished article could begin, the human agents which dealt with that raw material and turned it into the finished product. Had property been well distributed, protected by co-operative guilds fenced round and supported by custom and by the autonomy of great artisan corporations, those accumulations of wealth, necessary for the launching of each new method of production and for each new perfection of it, would have been discovered in the mass of small owners. *Their* corporations, *their* little parcels of wealth combined would have furnished the *capitalisation* required for the new processes, and men already owners would, as one invention succeeded another, have increased the total wealth of the community without disturbing the balance of distribution. There is no conceivable link in reason or in experience which binds the capitalisation of a new process with the idea of a few employing owners and a mass of employed non-owners working at a wage. Such great discoveries coming in a society like that of the thirteenth century would have blest and enriched mankind. Coming upon the diseased moral conditions of the eighteenth century in this country, they proved a curse.

To whom could the new industry turn for capitalisation? The small owner had already largely disappeared. The corporate life and mutual obligations which had supported him and confirmed him in his property had been broken to pieces by no "economic development," but by the deliberate action of the rich. He was ignorant because his schools had been taken from him and the universities closed to him. He was the more ignorant because the common life which once nourished his social sense and the co-operative arrangements which had once been his defence had disappeared. When you sought an accumulation of corn, of clothing, of housing, of fuel as the indispensable preliminary to the launching of your new industry; when you looked round for someone who could find the accumulated wealth necessary for these considerable experiments, you had to turn to the class which had already monopolised the bulk of the means of production in England. The rich men alone could furnish you with those supplies.

Nor was this all. The supplies once found and the adventure "capitalised," that form of human energy which lay best to hand, which was indefinitely exploitable, weak, ignorant, and desperately necessitous, ready to produce for you upon almost any terms, and glad enough if you would only keep it alive, was the existing proletariat which the new plutocracy had created when, in cornering the wealth of the country after the Reformation, they had thrust out the mass of Englishmen from the possession of implements, of houses, and of land.

The rich class, adopting some new process of production for its private gain, worked it upon those lines of mere competition which its avarice had already established. Co-operative tradition was dead. Where would it find its cheapest labour? Obviously among the proletariat—not among the remaining small owners. What class would increase under the new wealth? Obviously the proletariat again, without responsibilities, with nothing to leave to its progeny; and as they swelled the capitalist's gain, they enabled him with increasing power to buy out the small owner and send him to swell by another tributary the proletarian mass.

It was upon this account that the Industrial Revolution, as it is called, took in its very origins the form which has made it an almost unmixed curse for the unhappy society in which it has flourished. The rich. already possessed of the accumulations by which that industrial change could alone be nourished, inherited all its succeeding accumulations of implements and all its increasing accumulations of subsistence. The factory system, starting upon a basis of capitalist and proletariat, grew in the mould which had determined its origins. With every new advance the capitalist looked for proletariat grist to feed the productive mill. Every circumstance of that society, the form in which the laws that governed ownership and profit were cast, the obligations of partners, the relations between "master" and "man," directly made for the indefinite expansion of a subject, formless, wage-earning class controlled by a small body of owners, which body would tend to become smaller and richer still, and to be possessed of power ever greater and greater as the bad business unfolded.

The spread of economic oligarchy was everywhere, and not in industry alone. The great landlords destroyed deliberately and of set purpose and to their own advantage the common rights over common land. The small plutocracy with which they were knit up, and with whose mercantile elements they were now fused, directed everything to its own ends. That strong central government which should protect the community against the rapacity of a few had gone generations before. Capitalism triumphant wielded all the mechanism of legislation and of information too. It still holds them; and there is not an example of so-called "Social Reform" to-day which is not demonstrably (though often subconsciously) directed to the further entrenchment and confirmation of an industrial society in which it is taken for granted that a few shall own, that the vast majority shall live at a wage under them, and that all the bulk of Englishmen may hope for is the amelioration of their lot by regulations and by control from above but not by property; not by freedom.

We all feel—and those few of us who have analysed

the matter not only feel but know—that the Capitalist society thus gradually developed from its origins in the capture of the land four hundred years ago has reached its term. It is almost self-evident that it cannot continue in the form which now three generations have known, and it is equally self-evident that some solution must be found for the intolerable and increasing instability with which it has poisoned our lives. But before considering the solutions variously presented by various schools of thought, I shall in my next section show how and why the English Capitalist Industrial System is thus intolerably unstable and consequently presents an acute problem which must be solved under pain of social death.

It must be noted that modern Industrialism has spread to many other centres from England. It bears everywhere the features stamped upon it by its origin in this country.

SECTION FIVE

THE CAPITALIST STATE IN PROPORTION AS IT GROWS PERFECT GROWS UNSTABLE

SECTION THE FIFTH
THE CAPITALIST STATE IN PROPORTION AS IT GROWS PERFECT GROWS UNSTABLE

From the historical digression which I have introduced by way of illustrating my subject in the last two sections I now return to the general discussion of my thesis and to the logical process by which it may be established.

The Capitalist State is unstable, and indeed more properly a transitory phase lying between two permanent and stable states of society.

In order to appreciate why this is so, let us recall the definition of the Capitalist State:—

"A society in which the ownership of the means of production is confined to a body of free citizens, not large enough to make up properly a general character of that society, while the rest are dispossessed of the means of production, and are therefore proletarian, we call *Capitalist*."

Note the several points of such a state of affairs. You have private ownership; but it is not private ownership distributed in many hands and thus familiar as an institution to society as a whole. Again, you have the great majority dispossessed but at the same time citizens, that is, men politically free to act, though economically impotent; again, though it is but an inference from our definition, it is a necessary inference that there will be under Capitalism a conscious, direct, and planned *exploitation* of the majority, the free citizens who do not own by the minority who are owners. For wealth must be produced: the whole of that community must live: and the possessors can make such terms with the non-possessors as shall make it certain that a portion of what the non-possessors have produced shall go to the possessors.

A society thus constituted cannot endure. It cannot endure because it is subject to two very severe strains: strains which increase in severity in proportion as that society becomes more thoroughly Capitalist. The first of these strains arises from the divergence between the moral theories upon which the State reposes and the social facts which those moral theories attempt to govern. The second strain arises from the insecurity to which Capitalism condemns the great mass of society, and the general character of anxiety and peril which it imposes upon all citizens, but in particular upon the majority, which consists, under Capitalism, of dispossessed free men.

Of these two strains it is impossible to say which is the gravest. Either would be enough to destroy a social arrangement in which it was long present. The two combined make that destruction certain; and there is no longer any doubt that Capitalist society must transform itself into some other and more stable arrangement. It is the object of these pages to discover what that stable arrangement will probably be.

We say that there is a moral strain already intolerably severe and growing more severe with every perfection of Capitalism.

This moral strain comes from a contradiction between the realities of Capitalist and the moral base of our laws and traditions.

The moral base upon which our laws are still administered and our conventions raised presupposes a state composed of free citizens. Our laws defend property as a normal institution with which all citizens are acquainted, and which all citizens respect. It punishes theft as an abnormal incident only occurring when, through evil motives, one free citizen acquires the property of another without his knowledge and against his will. It punishes fraud as another abnormal incident in which, from evil motives, one free citizen induces another to part with his property upon false representations. It enforces contract, the sole moral base of which is the freedom of the two contracting parties, and the power of either, if it so please him, not to enter into a contract which, once entered into, must be enforced. It gives to an owner the power to leave his property by will, under the conception that such ownership and such passage of property (to natural heirs as a rule, but exceptionally to any other whom the testator may point out) is the normal operation of a society generally familiar with such things, and finding them part of the domestic life lived by the mass of its citizens. It casts one citizen in damages if by any willful action he has caused loss to another—for it presupposes him able to pay.

The sanction upon which social life reposes is, in

our moral theory, the legal punishment enforceable in our Courts, and the basis presupposed for the security and material happiness of our citizens is the possession of goods which shall guarantee us from anxiety and permit us an independence of action in the midst of our fellowmen.

Now contrast all this, the moral theory upon which society is still perilously conducted, the moral theory to which Capitalism itself turns for succour when it is attacked, contrast, I say, its formulae and its presuppositions with the social reality of a Capitalist State such as is England to-day.

Property remains as an instinct perhaps with most of the citizens; as an experience and a reality it is unknown to nineteen out of twenty. One hundred forms of fraud, the necessary corollary of unrestrained competition between a few and of unrestrained avarice as the motive controlling production, are not or cannot be punished: petty forms of violence in theft and of cunning in fraud the laws can deal with, but they cannot deal with these alone. Our legal machinery has become little more than an engine for protecting the few owners against the necessities, the demands, or the hatred of the mass of their dispossessed fellow-citizens. The vast bulk of so-called "free" contracts are to-day leonine contracts: arrangements which one man was free to take or to leave, but which the other man was not free to take or to leave, because the second had for his alternative starvation.

Most important of all, the fundamental social fact of

our movement, far more important than any security afforded by law, or than any machinery which the State can put into action, is the fact that *livelihood* is at the will of the possessors. It can be granted by the possessors to the non-possessors, or it can be withheld. The real sanction in our society for the arrangements by which it is conducted is not punishment enforceable by the Courts, but the withholding of livelihood from the dispossessed by the possessors. Most men now fear the loss of employment more than they fear legal punishment, and the discipline under which men are coerced in their modern forms of activity in England is the fear of dismissal. The true master of the Englishman to-day is not the Sovereign nor the officers of State, nor, save indirectly, the laws; his true master is the Capitalist.

Of these main truths everyone is aware; and anyone who sets out to deny them does so to-day at the peril of his reputation either for honesty or for intelligence.

If it be asked why things have come to a head so late (Capitalism having been in growth for so long), the answer is that England, even now the most completely Capitalist State of the modern world, did not itself become a completely Capitalist State until the present generation. Within the memory of men now living half England was agricultural, with relations domestic rather than competitive between the various human factors to production.

This moral strain, therefore, arising from the divergence between what our laws and moral phrases pretend, and what our society actually is, makes of, that society an utterly unstable thing.

This spiritual thesis is of far greater gravity than the narrow materialism of a generation now passing might imagine. Spiritual conflict is more fruitful of instability in the State than conflict of any other kind, and there is acute spiritual conflict, conflict in every man's conscience and ill-ease throughout the commonwealth when the realities of society are divorced from the moral base of its institution.

The second strain which we have noted in Capitalism, its second element of instability, consists in the fact that Capitalism destroys security.

Experience is enough to save us any delay upon this main point of our matter. But even without experience we could reason with absolute certitude from the very nature of Capitalism that its chief effect would be the destruction of security in human life.

Combine these two elements: the ownership of the means of production by a very few; the political freedom of owners and non-owners alike. There follows immediately from that combination a competitive market wherein the labour of the non-owner fetches just what it is worth, not as full productive power, but as productive power which will leave a surplus to the Capitalist. It fetches nothing when the labourer cannot work, more in proportion to the pace at which he is driven; less in middle age than in youth; less in old age than in middle age; nothing in sickness; nothing in despair.

A man in a position to accumulate (the normal result of human labour), a man founded upon property in sufficient amount and in established form is no more productive in his non-productive moments than is a proletarian; but his life is balanced and regulated by his reception of rent and interest as well as wages. Surplus values come to him, and are the fly-wheel balancing the extremes of his life and carrying him over his bad times. With a proletarian it cannot be so. The aspect from Capital looks at a human being whose labour it proposes to purchase cuts right across that normal aspect of human life from which we all regard our own affections, duties, and character. A man thinks of himself, of his chances and of his security along the line of his own individual existence from birth to death. Capital purchasing his labour (and not the man himself) purchases but a cross-section of his life, his moments of activity. For the rest, he must fend for himself; but to fend for yourself when you have nothing is to starve.

As a matter of fact, where a few possess the means of production perfectly free political conditions are impossible. A perfect Capitalist State cannot exist, though we have come nearer to it in modern England than other and more fortunate nations had thought possible. In the perfect Capitalist State there would be no food available for the non-owner save when he was actually engaged in Production, and that absurdity would, by quickly ending all human lives save those of the owners, put a term to the arrangement. If you left men completely free under a Capitalist system, there would be so heavy a mortality from starvation as would dry up the sources of labour in a very short time.

Imagine the dispossessed to be ideally perfect cowards, the possessors to consider nothing whatsoever except the buying of their labour in the cheapest market—and the system would break down from the death of children and of out-o'-works and of women. You would not have a State in mere decline such as ours is. You would have a State manifestly and patently perishing.

As a fact, of course, Capitalism cannot proceed to its own logical extreme. So long as the political freedom of all citizens is granted [the freedom of the few possessors of food to grant or withhold it, of the many non-possessors to strike any bargain at all, lest they lack it]: to exercise such freedom fully is to starve the very young, the old, the impotent, and the despairing to death. Capitalism must keep alive, by non-Capitalist methods, great masses of the population who would otherwise starve to death; and that is what Capitalism was careful to do to an increasing extent as it got a stronger and a stronger grip upon the English people. Elizabeth's Poor Law at the beginning of the business, the Poor Law of 1834, coming at a moment when nearly half England had passed into the grip of Capitalism, are original and primitive instances: there are to-day a hundred others.

Though this cause of insecurity—the fact that the possessors have no direct incentive to keep men alive—is logically the most obvious, and always the most enduring under a Capitalist system, there is another cause more poignant in its effect upon human life. That other cause is the competitive anarchy in production which restricted ownership coupled with freedom involves. Consider what is involved by the very process of production where the implements and the soil are in the hands of a few whose motive for causing the proletariat to produce is not the use of the wealth created but the enjoyment by those possessors of surplus value or "profit."

If full political freedom be allowed to any two such possessors of implements and stores, each will actively watch his market, attempt to undersell the other, tend to overproduce at the end of some season of extra demand for his article, thus glut the market only to suffer a period of depression afterwards and so forth. Again, the Capitalist, free, individual director of production, will miscalculate; sometimes he will fail, and his works will be shut down. Again, a mass of isolated, imperfectly instructed competing units cannot but direct their clashing efforts at an enormous waste, and that waste will fluctuate. Most commissions, most advertisements, most parades, are examples of this waste. If this waste of effort could be made a constant, the parasitical employment it afforded would be a constant too. But of its nature it is a most inconstant thing, and the employment it affords is therefore necessarily precarious. The concrete translation of this is the insecurity of the commercial traveller, the advertising agent, the insurance agent, and every form of touting and cozening which competitive Capitalism carries with it.

Now here again, as in the case of the insecurity produced by age and sickness, Capitalism cannot be pursued to its logical conclusion, and it is the element of freedom which suffers. Competition is, as a fact, restricted to an increasing extent by an understanding between the competitors, accompanied, especially in this country, by the ruin of the smaller competitor through secret conspiracies entered into by the larger men, and supported by the secret political forces of the State.* In a word, Capitalism, proving almost as unstable to the owners as to the non-owners, is tending towards stability by losing its essential character of political freedom. No better proof of the instability of Capitalism as a system could be desired.

Take any one of the numerous Trusts which now control English industry, and have made of modern England the type, quoted throughout the Continent, of artificial monopolies. If the full formula of Capitalism were accepted by our Courts and our executive statesmen, anyone could start a rival business, undersell those Trusts and shatter the comparative security they afford to industry within their field.

The reason that no one does this is that political freedom is not, as a fact, protected here by the Courts in commercial affairs. A man attempting to compete with one of our great English Trusts would find himself at once undersold. He might, by all the spirit of European

---

* Before any trust is established in this country, the first step is to "interest" one of our politicians. The Telephones, the South Wales Coal Trust, the happily defeated Soap Trust, the Soda, Fish, and Fruit Trusts, are examples in point.

law for centuries, indict those who would ruin him, citing them for a conspiracy in restraint of trade; of this conspiracy he would find the judge and the politicians most heartily in support.

But it must always be remembered that these conspiracies in restraint of trade which are the mark of modern England are in themselves a mark of the transition from the true Capitalist phase to another.

Under the essential conditions of Capitalism — under a perfect political freedom— such conspiracies would be punished by the Courts for what they are: to wit, a contravention of the fundamental doctrine of political liberty. For this doctrine, while it gives any man the right to make any contract he chooses with any labourer and offer the produce at such prices as he sees fit, also involves the protection of that liberty by the punishment of any conspiracy that may have monopoly for its object. If such perfect freedom is no longer attempted, if monopolies are permitted and fostered, it is because the unnatural strain to which freedom, coupled with restricted ownership, gives rise, the insecurity of its mere competition, the anarchy of its productive methods have at last proved intolerable.

I have already delayed more than was necessary in this section upon the causes which render a Capitalist State essentially unstable.

I might have treated the matter empirically, taking for granted the observation which all my readers must have made, that Capitalism is as a fact doomed, and that the Capitalist State has already passed into its first phase of transition.

We are clearly no longer possessed of that absolutely political freedom which true Capitalism essentially demands. The insecurity involved, coupled with the divorce between our traditional morals and the facts of society, have already introduced such novel features as the permission of conspiracy among both possessors and non-possessors, the compulsory provision of security through State action, and all these reforms, implicit or explicit, the tendency of which I am about to examine.

SECTION SIX

THE STABLE SOLUTIONS OF THIS INSTABILITY

SECTION THE SIXTH
THE STABLE SOLUTIONS OF THIS INSTABILITY

Given a Capitalist State, of its nature unstable, it will tend to reach stability by some method or another.

It is the definition of unstable equilibrium that a body in unstable equilibrium is seeking a stable equilibrium. For instance, a pyramid balanced upon its apex is in unstable equilibrium; which simply means that a slight force one way or the other will make it fall into a position where it will repose. Similarly, certain chemical mixtures are said to be in unstable equilibrium when their constituent parts have such affinity one for another that a slight shock may make them combine and transform the chemical arrangement of the whole. Of this sort are explosives.

If the Capitalist State is in unstable equilibrium, this only means that it is seeking a stable equilibrium, and that Capitalism cannot but be transformed into some other arrangement wherein Society may repose.

There are but three social arrangements which can replace Capitalism: Slavery, Socialism, and Property.

I may imagine a mixture of any two of these three or of all the three, but each is a dominant type, and from the very nature of the problem no fourth arrangement can be devised.

The problem turns, remember, upon the control of the means of production. Capitalism means that this control is vested in the hands of few, while political freedom is the appanage of all. If this anomaly cannot endure, from its insecurity and from its own contradiction with its presumed moral basis, you must either have a transformation of the one or of the other of the two elements which combined have been found unworkable. These two factors are (*1*) The ownership of the means of Production by a few; (*2*) The Freedom of all. To solve Capitalism you must get rid of restricted ownership, or of freedom, or of both. Now there is only one alternative to freedom, which is the negation of it. Either a man is free to work and not to work as he pleases, or he may be liable to a legal compulsion to work, backed by the forces of the State. In the first he is a free man; in the second he is by definition a slave. We have, therefore, so far as this factor of freedom is concerned, no choice between a number of changes, but only the opportunity of one, to wit, the establishment of slavery in place of freedom. Such a solution, the direct, immediate, and conscious re-establishment of slavery, would provide a true solution of the problems which Capitalism offers. It would guarantee, under workable regulations, sufficiency and security for the dispossessed. Such a solution, as I shall show, is the probable goal which our society will in fact approach. To its immediate and conscious acceptance, however, there is an obstacle.

A direct and conscious establishment of slavery as a solution to the problem of Capitalism, the surviving Christian tradition of our civilisation compels men to reject. No reformer will advocate it; no prophet dares take it as yet for granted. All theories of a reformed society will therefore attempt, at first, to leave untouched the factor of *Freedom* among the elements which make up Capitalism, and will concern themselves with some change in the factor of *Property.*[*]

Now, in attempting to remedy the evils of Capitalism by remedying that one of its two factors which consists in an ill distribution of property, you have two, and only two, courses open to you.

If you are suffering because property is restricted to a few, you can alter that factor in the problem *either* by putting property into the hands of many, *or* by putting it into the hands of none. There is no third course.

In the concrete, to put property in the hands of "none" means to vest it as a trust in the hands of political officers. If you say that the evils proceeding from Capitalism are due to the institution of property itself, and not to the dispossession of the many by the few, then you must forbid the private possession of the means of production by any particular and private part of the community: but someone must control the means of production, or we should have nothing to eat. So in practice this doctrine means the management of the means of production by those who are the public officers of the community. Whether these public officers are themselves controlled by the community or no has nothing to do with this solution on its economic side. The essential point to grasp is that the only alternative to

---

* By which word "*property*" is meant, of course, property in the means of Production.

private property is public property. Somebody must see to the ploughing and must control the ploughs; otherwise no ploughing will be done.

It is equally obvious that if you conclude property in itself to be no evil but only the small number of its owners, then your remedy is to increase the number of those owners.

So much being grasped, we may recapitulate and say that a society like ours, disliking the name of "slavery," and avoiding a direct and conscious re-establishment of the slave status, will necessarily contemplate the reform of its ill-distributed ownership on one of two models. The first is the negation of private property and the establishment of what is called Collectivism: that is, the management of the means of production by the political officers of the community. The second is the wider distribution of property until that institution shall become the mark of the whole State, and until free citizens are normally found to be possessors of capital or land, or both.

The first model we call *Socialism* or the Collectivist State; the second we call the Proprietary or Distributive State.

With so much elucidated, I will proceed to show in my next section why the second model, involving the redistribution of property, is rejected as impracticable by our existing Capitalist Society, and why, therefore, the model chosen by reformers is the first model, that of a Collectivist State.

I shall then proceed to show that at its first inception all Collectivist Reform is necessarily deflected and evolves, in the place of what it had intended, a new thing: a society wherein the owners remain few and wherein the proletarian mass accepts security at the expense of servitude.

Have I made myself clear?

If not, I will repeat for the third time, and in its briefest terms, the formula which is the kernel of my whole thesis.

The Capitalist State breeds a Collectivist Theory which in *action* produces something utterly different from Collectivism: to wit, the SERVILE STATE.

SECTION SEVEN

SOCIALISM IS THE EASIEST APPARENT SOLUTION OF THE CAPITALIST CRUX

SECTION THE SEVENTH
SOCIALISM THE EASIEST APPARENT SOLUTION OF THE CAPITALIST CRUX

I say that the line of least resistance, if it be followed, leads a Capitalist State to transform itself into a Servile State.

I propose to show that this comes about from the fact that not a *Distributive* but a *Collectivist* solution is the easiest for a Capitalist State to aim at, and that yet, in the very act of attempting *Collectivism*, what results is not Collectivism at all, but the servitude of the many, and the confirmation in their present privilege of the few; that is, the Servile State.

Men to whom the institution of slavery is abhorrent propose for the remedy of Capitalism one of two reforms.

Either they would put property into the hands of most citizens, so dividing land and capital that a determining number of families in the State were possessed of the means of production; or they would put those means of production into the hands of the political officers of the community, to be held in trust for the advantage of all.

The first solution may be called the attempted establishment of the DISTRIBUTIVE STATE. The second may be called the attempted establishment of the COLLECTIVIST STATE.

Those who favour the first course are the Conservatives or Traditionalists. They are men who respect and would, if possible, preserve the old forms of Christian European life. They know that property was thus distributed throughout the State during the happiest periods of our past history; they also know that where it is properly distributed to-day, you have greater social sanity and ease than elsewhere. In general, those who would re-establish, if possible, the Distributive State in the place of, and as a remedy for, the vices and unrest of Capitalism, are men concerned with known realities, and having for their ideal a condition of society which experience has tested and proved both stable and good. They are then, of the two schools of reformers, the more *practical* in the sense that they deal more than do the Collectivists (called also Socialists) with things which either are or have been in actual existence. But they are less practical in another sense (as we shall see in a moment) from the fact that the stage of the disease with which they are dealing does not readily lend itself to such a reaction as they propose.

The Collectivist, on the other hand, proposes to put land and capital into the hands of the political officers of the community, and this on the understanding that they shall hold such land and capital in trust for the advantage of the community. In making this proposal he is evidently dealing with a state of things hitherto imaginary, and his ideal is not one that has been tested by experience, nor one of which our race and history can furnish instances. In this sense, therefore, he is the *less* practical of the two reformers. His ideal cannot be discovered in any past, known, and recorded phase of our society. We cannot examine Socialism in actual working, nor can we say (as we can say of well-divided property): "On such and such an occasion, in such and such a period of European history, Collectivism was established and produced both stability and happiness in society."

In this sense, therefore, the Collectivist is far less practical than the reformer who desires well-distributed property.

On the other hand, there is a sense in which this Socialist is more practical than that other type of reformer, from the fact that the stage of the disease into which we have fallen apparently admits of his remedy with less shock than it admits of a reaction towards well-divided property.

For example: the operation of buying out some great tract of private ownership to-day (as a railway or a harbour company) with public funds, continuing its administration by publicly paid officials and converting its revenue to public use, is a thing with which we are familiar and which seemingly might be indefinitely multiplied. Individual examples of such transformation of waterworks, gas, tramways, from a Capitalist to a Collectivist basis are common, and the change does not disturb any fundamental thing in our society. When a private Water company or Tramway line is bought by some town and worked thereafter in the interests of the public, the transaction is effected without any perceptible friction, disturbs the life of no private citizen, and seems in every way normal to the society in which it takes place.

Upon the contrary, the attempt to create a large number of share holders in such enterprises and artificially to substitute many partners, distributed throughout a great number of the population, in the place of the original few capitalist owners, would prove lengthy and at every step would arouse opposition, would create disturbance, would work at an expense of great friction, and would be imperilled by the power of the new and many owners to sell again to a few.

In a word, the man who desires to re-establish property as an institution normal to most citizens in the State is working *against* the grain of our existing Capitalist society, while a man who desires to establish Socialism—that is Collectivism—is working *with* the grain of that society. The first is like a physician who should say to a man whose limbs were partially atrophied from disuse: "Do this and that, take such and such exercise, and you will recover the use of your limbs." The second is like a physician who should say: "You cannot go on as you are. Your limbs are atrophied from lack of use. Your attempt to conduct yourself as though they were not is useless and painful; you had better make up your mind to be wheeled about in a fashion consonant to your disease." The Physician is the Reformer, his Patient the Proletariat.

It is not the purpose of this book to show how and under what difficulties a condition of well-divided property might be restored and might take the place (even in England) of that Capitalism which is now no longer either stable or tolerable; but for the purposes of contrast and to emphasise my argument I will proceed, before showing how the Collectivist unconsciously makes for the Servile State, to show what difficulties surround the Distributive solution and why, therefore, the Collectivist solution appeals so much more readily to men living under Capitalism.

If I desire to substitute a number of small owners for a few large ones in some particular enterprise, how shall I set to work?

I might boldly confiscate and redistribute at a blow. But by what process should I choose the new owners? Even supposing that there was some machinery whereby the justice of the new distribution could be assured, how could I avoid the enormous and innumerable separate acts of injustice that would attach to general redistributions? To say "none shall own" and to confiscate is one thing; to say "all should own" and apportion ownership is another. Action of this kind would so disturb the whole network of economic relations as to bring ruin at once to the whole body politic, and particularly to the smaller interests indirectly affected. In a society such as ours a catastrophe falling upon the State from outside might indirectly do good by making such a redistribution possible. But no one working from within the State could provoke that catastrophe without ruining his own cause.

If, then, I proceed more slowly and more rationally and canalise the economic life of society so that small property shall gradually be built up within it, see against what forces of inertia and custom I have to work to-day in a Capitalist society!

If I desire to benefit small savings at the expense of large, I must reverse the whole economy under which interest is paid upon deposits to-day. It is far easier to save £100 out of a revenue of £1000 than to save 10 out of a revenue of 100. It is infinitely easier to save £10 out of a revenue of £100 than £5 out of a revenue of £50. To build up small property through thrift when once the Mass have fallen into the proletarian trough is impossible unless you deliberately subsidise small savings, offering them a reward which, incompetition, they could never obtain; and to do this the whole vast arrangement of credit must be worked backwards. Or, let the policy be pursued of penalising undertakings with few owners, of heavily taxing large blocks of shares and of subsidising with the produce small holders in proportion to the smallness of their holding. Here again you are met with the difficulty of a vast majority who cannot even bid for the smallest share.

One might multiply instances of the sort indefinitely, but the strongest force against the distribution of ownership in a society already permeated with Capitalist modes of thought is still the moral one: Will men want to own? Will officials, administrators, and law-makers be able to shake off the power which under Capitalism seems normal to the rich? If I approach, for instance, the works of one of our great Trusts, purchase it with public money, bestow, even as a gift, the shares thereof to its workmen, can I count upon any tradition of property in their midst which will prevent their squandering the new wealth? Can I discover any relics of the co-operative instinct among such men? Could I get managers and organisers to take a group of poor men seriously or to serve them as they would serve rich men? Is not the whole psychology of a Capitalist society divided between the proletarian mass which thinks in terms not of property but of "employment," and the few owners who are alone familiar with the machinery of administration?

I have touched but very briefly and superficially upon this matter, because it needs no elaboration. Though it is evident that with a sufficient will and a sufficient social vitality property could be restored, it is evident that all efforts to restore it have in a Capitalist society such as our own a note of oddity, of doubtful experiment, of being unco-ordinated with other social things around them, which marks the heavy handicap under which any such attempt must proceed. It is like recommending elasticity to the aged.

On the other hand, the Collectivist experiment is thoroughly suited (in appearance at least) to the Capitalist society which it proposes to replace. It works with the existing machinery of Capitalism, talks and thinks in the existing terms of Capitalism, appeals to just those appetites which Capitalism has aroused, and ridicules as fantastic and unheard-of just those things in society the memory of which Capitalism has killed among men wherever the blight of it has spread.

So true is all this that the stupider kind of Collectivist will often talk of a "Capitalist phase" of society as the necessary precedent to a "Collectivist phase." A trust or monopoly is welcomed because it "furnishes a mode of transition from private to public ownership." Collectivism promises employment to the great mass who think of production only in terms of employment. It promises to its workmen the security which a great and well-organised industrial Capitalist unit (like one of our railways) can give through a system of pensions, regular promotion, etc., but that security vastly increased through the fact that it is the State and not a mere unit of the State which guarantees it. Collectivism would administer, would pay wages, would promote, would pension off, would fine—and all the rest of it—exactly as the Capitalist State does to-day. The proletarian, when the Collectivist (or Socialist) State is put before him, perceives nothing in the picture save certain ameliorations of his present position. Who can imagine that if, say, two of our great industries, Coal and Railways, were handed over to the State to-morrow, the armies of men organised therein would find any change in the character of their lives, save in some increase of security and possibly in a very slight increase of earnings?

The whole scheme of Collectivism presents, so far as the proletarian mass of a Capitalist State is concerned, nothing unknown at all, but a promise of some increment in wages and a certainty of far greater ease of mind.

To that small minority of a Capitalist society which owns the means of production, Collectivism will of course appear as an enemy, but, even so, it is an enemy which they understand and an enemy with whom they can treat in terms common both to that enemy and to themselves. If, for instance, the State proposes to take over such and such a trust now paying 4 percent, and believes that under State management it will make the trust pay 5 per cent., then the transference takes the form of a business proposition : the State is no harder to the Capitalists taken over than was Mr. Yerkes to the Underground. Again, the State, having greater credit and longevity, can (it would seem)* "buy out" any existing Capitalist body upon favourable terms. Again, the discipline by which the State would enforce its rules upon the proletariat it employed would be the same rules as those by which the Capitalist imposes discipline in his own interests to-day.

There is in the whole scheme which proposes to transform the Capitalist into the Collectivist State no element of reaction, the use of no term with which a Capitalist society is not familiar, the appeal to no instinct, whether of cowardice, greed, apathy, or mechanical regulation, with which a Capitalist community is not amply familiar.

In general, if modern Capitalist England were made by magic a State of small owners, we should all suffer an enormous revolution. We should marvel at the insolence of the poor, at the laziness of the contented, at the strange diversities of task, at the rebellious, vigorous personalities discernible upon every side. But if this

* That this is an illusion I shall attempt to show on a later page.

modern Capitalist England could, by a process sufficiently slow to allow for the readjustment of individual interests, be transformed into a Collectivist State, the apparent change at the end of that transition would not be conspicuous to the most of us, and the transition itself should have met with no shocks that theory can discover. The insecure and hopeless margin below the regularly paid ranks of labour would have disappeared into isolated workplaces of a penal kind: we should hardly miss them. Many incomes now involving considerable duties to the State would have been replaced by incomes as large or larger, involving much the same duties and bearing only the newer name of salaries. The small shop-keeping class would find itself in part absorbed under public schemes at a salary, in part engaged in the old work of distribution at secure incomes; and such small owners as are left, of boats, of farms, even of machinery, would perhaps know the new state of things into which they had survived through nothing more novel than some increase in the irritating system of inspection and of onerous petty taxation: they are already fairly used to both.

This picture of the natural transition from Capitalism to Collectivism seems so obvious that many Collectivists in a generation immediately past believed that nothing stood between them and the realisation of their ideal save the unintelligence of mankind. They had only to argue and expound patiently and systematically for the great transformation to become possible. They had only to continue arguing and expounding for it at last to be realised.

I say, "of the last generation." To-day that simple and superficial judgment is getting woefully disturbed. The most sincere and single-minded of Collectivists cannot but note that the practical effect of their propaganda is not an approach towards the Collectivist State at all, but towards something very different. It is becoming more and more evident that with every new reform—and those reforms commonly promoted by particular Socialists, and in a puzzled way blessed by Socialists in general—another state emerges more and more clearly. It is becoming increasingly certain that the attempted transformation of Capitalism into Collectivism is resulting not in Collectivism at all, but in some third thing which the Collectivist never dreamt of, or the Capitalist either; and that third thing is the SERVILE State: a State, that is, in which the mass of men shall be constrained *by law* to labour to the profit of a minority, but, as the price of such constraint, shall enjoy a security which the old Capitalism did not give them.

Why is the apparently simple and direct action of Collectivist reform diverted into so unexpected a channel? And in what new laws and institutions does modern England in particular and industrial society in general show that this new form of the State is upon us?

To these two questions I will attempt an answer in the two concluding divisions of this book.

SECTION EIGHT

THE REFORMERS AND THE REFORMED ARE ALIKE MAKING FOR THE SERVILE STATE

SECTION EIGHT
THE REFORMERS AND THE REFORMED ARE ALIKE MAKING FOR THE SERVILE STATE

I propose in this section to show how the three interests which between them account for nearly the whole of the forces making for social change in modern England are all necessarily drifting towards the Servile State.

Of these three interests the first two represent the Reformers—the third the people to be Reformed.

These three interests are, first, the *Socialist*, who is the theoretical reformer working along the line of least resistance; secondly, the "*Practical Man*" who as a "practical" reformer depends on his shortness of sight, and is therefore to-day a powerful factor; while the third is that great proletarian mass for whom the change is being effected, and on whom it is being imposed. What *they* are most likely to accept, the way in which *they* will react upon new institutions is the most important factor of all, for they are the material with and upon which the work is being done.

(1) Of the Socialist Reformer:

I say that men attempting to achieve Collectivism or Socialism as the remedy for the evils of the Capitalist State find themselves drifting not towards a Collectivist State at all, but towards a Servile State.

The Socialist movement, the first of the three factors in this drift, is itself made up of two kinds of men: there is (*a*) the man who regards the public ownership of the means of production (and the consequent compulsion of all citizens to work under the direction of the State) as the only feasible solution of our modern social ills. There is also (*b*) the man who loves the Collectivist ideal in itself, who does not pursue it so much because it is a solution of modern Capitalism, as because it is an ordered and regular form of society which appeals to him in itself. He loves to consider the ideal of a State in which land and capital shall be held by public officials who shall order other men about and so preserve them from the consequences of *their* vice, ignorance, and folly.

These types are perfectly distinct, in many respects antagonistic, and between them they cover the whole Socialist movement.

Now imagine either of these men at issue with the existing state of Capitalist society and attempting to transform it. Along what line of least resistance will either be led?

(*a*) The first type will begin by demanding the confiscation of the means of production from the hands of their present owners, and the vesting of them in the State. But wait a moment. That demand is an exceedingly hard thing to accomplish. The present owners have between them and confiscation a stony moral barrier. It is what *most* men would call the moral basis of property (the instinct that property is a *right*), and what all men would admit to be at least a deeply rooted tradition. Again, they have behind them the innumerable complexities of modern ownership.

To take a very simple case. Decree that all common lands enclosed since so late a date as 1760 shall revert to the public. There you have a very moderate case and a very defensible one. But conceive for a moment how many small freeholds, what a nexus of obligation and benefit spread over millions, what thousands of exchanges, what purchases made upon the difficult savings of small men such a measure would wreck! It is conceivable, for, in the moral sphere, society can do anything to society; but it would bring crashing down with it twenty times the wealth involved and all the secure credit of our community. In a word, the thing is, in the conversational use of that term, impossible. So your best type of Socialist reformer is led to an expedient which I will here only mention as it must be separately considered at length later on account of its fundamental importance the expedient of "*buying out*" the present owner.

It is enough to say in this place that the attempt to "buy out" without confiscation is based upon an economic error. This I shall prove in its proper place. For the moment I assume it and pass on to the rest of my reformer's action.

He does not confiscate, then; at the most he "buys out" (or attempts to "buy out") certain sections of the means of production.

But this action by no means covers the whole of his motive. By definition the man is out to cure what he sees to be the great immediate evils of Capitalist society. He is out to cure the destitution which it causes in great multitudes and the harrowing in- security which it imposes upon all. He is out to substitute for Capitalist society a society in which men shall all be fed, clothed, housed, and in which men shall not live in a perpetual jeopardy of their housing, clothing, and food.

Well, there is a way of achieving that without confiscation.

This reformer rightly thinks that the ownership of the means of production by a few has caused the evils which arouse his indignation and pity. But they have only been so caused on account of a combination of such limited ownership with universal freedom. The combination of the two is the very definition of the Capitalist State. It is difficult indeed to dispossess the possessors. It is by no means so difficult (as we shall see again when we are dealing with the mass whom these changes will principally affect) to modify the factor of freedom.

You can say to the Capitalist: "I desire to dispossess you, and meanwhile I am determined that your employees shall live tolerable lives." The Capitalist replies: "I refuse to be dispossessed, and it is, short of catastrophe, impossible to dispossess me. But if you will define the relation between my employees and myself, I will undertake particular responsibilities due to my position. Subject the proletarian, as a proletarian, and because he is a proletarian, to special laws. Clothe me, the Capitalist, as a Capitalist, and because I am a

Capitalist, with special converse duties under those laws. I will faithfully see that they are obeyed; I will compel my employees to obey them, and I will undertake the new role imposed upon me by the State. Nay, I will go further, and I will say that such a novel arrangement will make my own profits perhaps larger and certainly more secure."

This idealist social reformer, therefore, finds the current of his demand canalised. As to one part of it, confiscation, it is checked and barred; as to the other, securing human conditions for the proletariat, the gates are open. Half the river is dammed by a strong weir, but there is a sluice, and that sluice can be lifted. Once lifted, the whole force of the current will run through the opportunity so afforded it; there will it scour and deepen its channel; there will the main stream learn to run.

To drop the metaphor, all those things in the true Socialist's demand which are compatible with the Servile State can certainly be achieved. The first steps towards them are already achieved. They are of such a nature that upon them can be based a further advance in the same direction, and the whole Capitalist State can be rapidly and easily transformed into the Servile State, satisfying in its transformation the more immediate claims and the more urgent demands of the social reformer whose ultimate objective indeed may be the public ownership of capital and land, but whose driving power is a burning pity for the poverty and peril of the masses.

When the transformation is complete there will be no ground left, nor any demand or necessity, for public ownership. The reformer only asked for it in order to secure security and sufficiency: he has obtained his demand.

Here are security and sufficiency achieved by another and much easier method, consonant with and proceeding from the Capitalist phase immediately preceding it: there is no need to go further.

In this way the Socialist whose motive is human good and not mere organisation is being shepherded in spite of himself *away* from his Collectivist ideal and towards a society in which the possessors shall remain possessed, the dispossessed shall remain dispossessed, in which the mass of men shall still work for the advantage of a few, and in which those few shall still enjoy the surplus values produced by labour, but in which the special evils of insecurity and insufficiency, in the main the product of freedom, have been eliminated by the destruction of freedom.

At the end of the process you will have two kinds of men, the owners economically free, and controlling to their peace and to the guarantee of their livelihood the economically unfree non-owners. But that is the Servile State.

(*b*) The second type of socialist reformer may be dealt with more briefly. In him the exploitation of man by man excites no indignation. Indeed, he is not of a type to which indignation or any other lively passion is familiar. Tables, statistics, an exact framework for life—these afford him the food that satisfies his moral apetite;

the occupation most congenial to him is the "running" of men: as a machine is run.

To such a man the Collectivist ideal particularly appeals.

It is orderly in the extreme. All that human and organic complexity which is the colour of any vital society offends him by its infinite differentiation. He is disturbed by multitudinous things; and the prospect of a vast bureaucracy wherein the whole of life shall be scheduled and appointed to certain simple schemes deriving from the co-ordinate work of public clerks and marshalled by powerful heads of departments gives his small stomach a final satisfaction.

Now this man, like the other, would prefer to begin with public property in capital and land, and upon that basis to erect the formal scheme which so suits his peculiar temperament. (It need hardly be said that in his vision of a future society he conceives of himself as the head of at least a department and possibly of the whole State—but that is by the way.) But while he would prefer to begin with a Collectivist scheme ready-made, he finds in practice that he cannot do so. He would have to confiscate just as the more hearty Socialist would; and if that act is very difficult to the man burning at the sight of human wrongs. how much more difficult is it to a man impelled by no such motive force and directed by nothing more intense than a mechanical appetite for regulation?

He cannot confiscate or begin to confiscate. At the

best he will "buy out" the Capitalist.

Now, in his case, as in the case of the more human Socialist, "buying out" is, as I shall show in its proper place, a system impossible of general application.

But all those other things for which such a man cares much more than he does for the socialisation of the means of production—tabulation, detailed administration of men, the co-ordination of many efforts under one schedule, the elimination of all private power to react against his Department, all these are immediately obtainable without disturbing the existing arrangement of society. With him, precisely as with the other socialist, what he desires can be reached without any dispossession of the few existing possessors. He has but to secure the registration of the proletariat; next to ensure that neither they in the exercise of their freedom, nor the employer in the exercise of his, can produce insufficiency or insecurity—and he is content. Let laws exist which make the proper housing, feeding, clothing, and recreation of the proletarian mass be incumbent upon the possessing class, and the observance of such rules be imposed, by inspection and punishment, upon those whom he pretends to benefit, and all that he really cares for will be achieved.

To such a man the Servile State is hardly a thing towards which he drifts, it is rather a tolerable alternative to his ideal Collectivist State, which alternative he is quite prepared to accept and regards favourably. Already the greater part of such reformers who, a generation ago, would have called themselves "Socialists" are now less concerned with any scheme for socialising Capital and Land than with innumerable schemes actually existing, some of them possessing already the force of laws, for regulating, "running," and drilling the protelariat without trenching by an inch upon the privilege in implements, stores, and land enjoyed by the small Capitalist class.

The so-called "Socialist" of this type has not fallen into the Servile State by a miscalculation. He has fathered it; he welcomes its birth, he foresees his power over its future.

So much for the Socialist movement, which a generation ago proposed to transform our Capitalist society into one where the community should be the universal owner and all men equally economically free or unfree under its tutelage. To-day their ideal has failed, and of the two sources whence their energy proceeded, the one is reluctantly, the other gladly, acquiescent in the advent of a society which is not Socialist at all but Servile.

(2) Of the *Practical* Reformer:

There is another type of Reformer, one who prides himself on not being a socialist, and one of the greatest weight to-day. He also is making for the Servile State. This second factor in the change is the "Practical Man"; and this fool, on account of his great numbers and determining influence in the details of legislation, must be carefully examined.

It is your "Practical Man" who says: "Whatever you theorists and doctrinaires may hold with regard to this proposal (which I support), though it may offend some abstract dogma of yours, yet *in practice* you must admit that it does good. If you had *practical* experience of the misery of the Jones' family, or had done *practical* work yourself in Pudsey, you would have seen that a *practical* man," etc.

It is not difficult to discern that the Practical Man in social reform is exactly the same animal as the Practical Man in every other department of human energy, and may be discovered suffering from the same twin disabilities which stamp the Practical Man where-ever found: these twin disabilities are an inability to define his own first principles and an inability to follow the consequences proceeding from his own action. Both these disabilities proceed from one simple and deplorable form of impotence, the inability to think.

Let us help the Practical Man in his weakness and do a little thinking for him.

As a social reformer he has of course (though he does not know it) first principles and dogmas like all the rest of us, and *his* first principles and dogmas are exactly the same as those which his intellectual superiors hold in the matter of social reform. The two things intolerable to him as a decent citizen (though a very stupid human being) are *insufficiency* and *insecurity*. When he was "working" in the slums of Pudsey or raiding the proletarian Jones's from the secure base of Toynbee Hall, what shocked the worthy man most was "unemployment" and "destitution": that is, insecurity and insufficiency in flesh and blood.

Now, if the Socialist who has thought out his case, whether as a mere organiser or as a man hungering and thirsting after justice, is led away from Socialism and towards the Servile State by the force of modern things in England, how much more easily do you not think the "Practical Man" will be conducted towards that same Servile State, like any donkey to his grazing ground? To those dull and short-sighted eyes the immediate solution which even the beginnings of the Servile State propose are what a declivity is to a piece of brainless matter. The piece of brainless matter rolls down the declivity, and the Practical Man lollops from Capitalism to the Servile State with the same inevitable ease. Jones has not got enough. If you give him something in charity, that something will be soon consumed, and then Jones will again not have enough. Jones has been seven weeks out of work. If you get him work "under our unorganised and wasteful system, etc.," he may lose it just as he lost his first jobs. The slums of Pudsey, as the Practical Man knows by Practical experience, are often unemployable. Then there are "the ravages of drink": more fatal still the dreadful habit mankind has of forming families and breeding children. The worthy fellow notes that "as a practical matter of fact such men do not work unless you make them."

He does not, because he cannot, co-ordinate all these things. He knows nothing of a society in which free men were once owners, nor of the co-operative and instinctive institutions for the protection of ownership which such a society spontaneously breeds. He "takes the world as he finds it" —and the consequence is that whereas men of greater capacity may admit with different degrees of reluctance the general principles of the Servile State, *he*, the Practical Man, positively gloats on every new detail in the building up of that form of society. And the destruction of freedom by inches (though he does not see it to be the destruction of freedom) is the one panacea so obvious that he marvels at the doctrinaires who resist or suspect the process.

It has been necessary to waste so much time on this deplorable individual because the circumstances of our generation give him a peculiar power. Under the conditions of modern exchange a man of that sort enjoys great advantages. He is to be found as he never was in any other society before our own, possessed of wealth, and political as never was any such citizen until our time. Of history with all its lessons; of the great schemes of philosophy and religion, of human nature itself he is blank.

The Practical Man left to himself would not produce the Servile State. He would not produce anything but a welter of anarchic restrictions which would lead at last to some kind of revolt.

Unfortunately, he is not left to himself. He is but the ally or flanking party of great forces which he does nothing to oppose, and of particular men, able and prepared for the work of general change, who use him with gratitude and contempt. Were he not so numerous in modern England, and, under the extraordinary conditions of a Capitalist State, so economically powerful, I would have neglected him in this analysis. As it is, we may console ourselves by remembering that the advent of the Servile State, with its powerful organisation and necessity for lucid thought in those who govern, will certainly eliminate him.

Our reformers, then, both those who think and those who do not, both those who are conscious of the process and those who are unconscious of it, are making directly for the Servile State.

(3) What of the third factor? What of the people about to be reformed? What of the millions upon whose carcasses the reformers are at work, and who are the subject of the great experiment? Do they tend, as material, to accept or to reject that transformation from free proletarianism to servitude which is the argument of this book?

The question is an important one to decide, for upon whether the material is suitable or unsuitable for the work to which it is subjected, depends the success of every experiment making for the Servile State.

The mass of men in the Capitalist State is proletarian. As a matter of definition, the actual number of the proletariat and the proportion that number bears to the total number of families in the State may vary, but must be sufficient to determine the general character of the State before we can call that State *Capitalist*.

But, as we have seen, the Capitalist State is not a stable, and therefore not a permanent, condition of society. It has proved ephemeral; and upon that very account the proletariat in any Capitalist State retains to a greater or less degree some memories of a state of society in which its ancestors were possessors of property and economically free.

The strength of this memory or tradition is the first element we have to bear in mind in our problem, when we examine how far a particular proletariat, such as the English proletariat to-day, is ready to accept the Servile State, which would condemn it to a perpetual loss of property and of all the free habit which property engenders.

Next be it noted that under conditions of freedom the Capitalist class may be entered by the more cunning or the more fortunate of the proletariat class. Recruitment of the kind was originally sufficiently common in the first development of Capitalism to be a standing feature in society and to impress the imagination of the general. Such recruitment is still possible. The proportion which it bears to the whole proletariat, the chance which each member of the proletariat may think he has of escaping from his proletarian condition in a particular phase of Capitalism such as is ours to-day, is the second factor in the problem.

The third factor, and by far the greatest of all, is the appetite of the dispossessed for that security and sufficiency of which Capitalism, with its essential condition of freedom, has deprived them.

Now let us consider the interplay of these three

factors in the English proletariat as we actually know it at this moment. That proletariat is certainly the, great mass of the State: it covers about nineteen- twentieths of the population if we exclude Ireland, where, as I shall point out in my concluding pages, the reaction against Capitalism, and therefore against its development towards a Servile State, is already successful.

As to the first factor, it has changed very rapidly within the memory of men now living. The traditional rights of property are still strong in the minds of the English poor. All the moral connotations of that right are familiar to them. They are familiar with the conception of theft as a wrong; they are tenacious of any scraps of property which they may acquire. They could all explain what is meant by ownership, by legacy, by exchange, and by gift, and even by contract. There is not one but could put himself in the position, mentally, of an owner.

But the actual experience of ownership, and the effect which that experience has upon character and upon one's view of the State is a very different matter. Within the memory of people still living a sufficient number of Englishmen were owning (as small freeholders, small masters, etc.) to give to the institution of property coupled with freedom a very vivid effect upon the popular mind. More than this, there was a living tradition proceeding from the lips of men who could still bear living testimony to the relics of a better state of things. I have myself spoken, when I was a boy, to old labourers in the neighbourhood of Oxford who had risked their skins in armed protest against the enclosure of certain commons, and who had of course suffered imprisonment by a wealthy judge as the reward of their courage; and I have my self spoken in Lancashire to old men who could retrace for me, either from their personal experience the last phases of small ownership in the textile trade, or, from what their fathers had told them, the conditions of a time when small and well-divided ownership in cottage looms was actually common.

All that has passed. The last chapter of its passage has been singularly rapid. Roughly speaking, it is the generation brought up under the Education Acts of the last forty years which has grown up definitely and hopelessly proletarian. The present instinct, use, and meaning of property is lost to it: and this has had two very powerful effects, each strongly inclining our modern wage-earners to ignore the old barriers which lay between a condition of servitude and a condition of freedom. The first effect is this: that property is no longer what they seek, nor what they think obtainable for themselves. The second effect is that they regard the possessors of property as a class apart, whom they always must ultimately obey, often envy, and sometimes hate; whose moral right to so singular a position most of them would hesitate to concede, and many of them would now strongly deny, but whose position they, at any rate, accept as a known and permanent social fact, the origins of which they have forgotten, and the foundations of which they believe to be immemorial.

To sum up: The attitude of the proletariat in England to-day (the attitude of the overwhelming majority, that is, of English families) towards property and towards that freedom which is alone obtainable through property is no longer an attitude of experience or of expectation. They think of themselves as wage-earners. To increase the weekly stipend of the wage-earner is an object which they vividly appreciate and pursue. To make him cease to be a wage- earner is an object that would seem to them entirely outside the realities of life.

What of the second factor, the gambling chance which the Capitalist system, with its necessary condition of freedom, of the legal power to bargain fully, and so forth, permits to the proletarian of escaping from his proletariat surroundings?

Of this gambling chance and the effect it has upon men's minds we may say that, while it has not disappeared, it has very greatly lost in force during the last forty years. One often meets men who tell one, whether they are speaking in defence of or against the Capitalist system, that it still blinds the proletarian to any common consciousness of class, because the proletarian still has the example before him of members of his class, whom he has known, rising (usually by various forms of villainy) to the position of capitalist. But when one goes down among the working men themselves, one discovers that the hope of such a change in the mind of any individual worker is now exceedingly remote. Millions of men in great groups of industry, notably in the transport industry and in the mines, have quite given up such an expectation. Tiny as the chance ever was, exaggerated as the hopes in a lottery always are, that tiny chance has fallen in the general opinion of the workers to be negligible, and that hope which a lottery breeds is extinguished. The proletarian now regards him- self as definitely proletarian, nor destined within human likelihood to be anything but proletarian.

These two factors, then, the memory of an older condition of economic freedom, and the effect of a hope individuals might entertain of escaping from the wage-earning class, the two factors which might act most strongly *against* the acceptation of the Servile State by that class, have so fallen in value that they offer but little opposition to the third factor in the situation which is making so strongly *for* the Servile State, and which consists in the necessity all men acutely feel for sufficiency and for security. It is this third factor alone which need be seriously considered to-day, when we ask ourselves how far the material upon which social reform is working, that is, the masses of the people, may be ready to accept the change.

The thing may be put in many ways. I will put it in what I believe to be the most conclusive of all.

If you were to approach those millions of families now living at a wage, with the proposal for a contract of service for life, guaranteeing them employment at what each regarded as his usual full wage, how many would refuse?

Such a contract would, of course, involve a loss of freedom: a life-contract of the kind is, to be accurate, no contract at all. It is the negation of contract and the acceptation of status. It would lay the man that undertook it under an obligation of forced labour, coterminous and coincident with his power to labour. It would be a permanent renunciation of his right (if such a right exists) to the surplus values created by his labour. If we ask ourselves how many men, or rather how many families, would prefer freedom (with its accompaniments of certain insecurity and possible insufficiency) to such a life-contract, no one can deny that the answer is: "Very few would refuse it." That is the key to the whole matter.

What proportion would refuse it no one can determine; but I say that even as a voluntary offer, and not as a compulsory obligation, a contract of this sort which would for the future destroy contract and re- erect status of a servile sort would be thought a boon by the mass of the proletariat to-day.

Now take the truth from another aspect—by considering it thus from one point of view and from another we can appreciate it best—Of what are the mass of men now most afraid in a Capitalist State? Not of the punishments that can be inflicted by a Court of Law, but of "the sack."

You may ask a man why he does not resist such and such a legal infamy; why he permits himself to be the victim of fines and deductions from which the Truck Acts specifically protect him; why he cannot assert his opinion in this or that matter; why he has accepted, without a blow, such and such an insult.

Some generations ago a man challenged to tell you why he forswore his manhood in any particular regard would have answered you that it was because he feared punishment at the hands of the law; to-day he will tell you that it is because he fears unemployment.

Private law has for the second time in our long European story overcome public law, and the sanctions which the Capitalist can call to the aid of his private rule, by the action of his private will, are stronger than those which the public Courts can impose.

In the seventeenth century a man feared to go to Mass lest the judges should punish him. To-day a, man fears to speak in favour of some social theory which he holds to be just and true lest his master should punish him. To deny the rule of public powers once involved public punishments which most men dreaded, though some stood out. To deny the rule of private powers involves to-day a private punishment against the threat of which very few indeed dare to stand out.

Look at the matter from yet another aspect. A law is passed (let us suppose) which increases the total revenue of a wage-earner, or guarantees him against the insecurity of his position in some small degree. The administration of that law requires, upon the one hand, a close inquisition into the man's circumstances by public officials, and, upon the other hand, the administration of its benefits by that particular Capitalist or group of Capitalists whom the wage-earner serves to enrich. Do the Servile conditions attaching to this material benefit prevent a proletarian in England to-day from preferring the benefit to freedom? It is notorious that they do not.

No matter from what angle you approach the business, the truth is always the same. That great mass of wage-earners upon which our society now reposes understands as a present good all that will increase even to some small amount their present revenue and all that may guarantee them against those perils of insecurity to which they are perpetually subject. They understand and welcome a good of this kind, and they are perfectly willing to pay for that good the corresponding price of control and enregimentation, exercised in gradually increasing degree by those who are their paymasters.

It would be easy by substituting superficial for fundamental things, or even by proposing certain terms and phrases to be used in the place of terms and phrases now current it would be easy, I say, by such methods to ridicule or to oppose the prime truths which I am here submitting. They none the less remain truths.

Substitute for the term "employee" in one of our new laws the term "serf," even do so mild a thing as to substitute the traditional term "master" for the word "employer," and the blunt words might breed revolt. Impose of a sudden the full conditions of a Servile State upon modern England, and it would certainly breed revolt. But my point is that when the foundations of the thing have to be laid and the first great steps taken, there is no revolt; on the contrary, there is acquiescence and for the most part gratitude upon the part of the poor. After the long terrors imposed upon them through a freedom unaccompanied by property, they see, at the expense of losing a mere legal freedom, the very real prospect of having *enough* and *not losing it.*

All forces, then, are making for the Servile State in this the final phase of our evil Capitalist society in England. The generous reformer is canalised towards it; the ungenerous one finds it a very mirror of his ideal; the herd of "practical" men meet at every stage in its inception the "practical" steps which they expected and demanded; while that proletarian mass upon whom the experiment is being tried have lost the tradition of property and of freedom which might resist the change, and are most powerfully inclined to its acceptance by the positive benefits which it confers.

It may be objected that however true all this may be, no one can, upon such theoretical grounds, regard the Servile State as something really approaching us. We need not believe in its advent (we shall be told) until we see the first effects of its action.

To this I answer that the first effects of its action are already apparent The Servile State is, in industrial England to-day, no longer a menace but something in actual existence. It is in process of construction. The first main lines of it are already plotted out; the corner-stone of it is already laid.

To see the truth of this it is enough to consider laws and projects of law, the first of which we already enjoy, while the last will pass from project to positive statute in due process of time.

APPENDIX ON "BUYING-OUT"

There is an impression abroad among those who pro- pose to expropriate the Capitalist class for the benefit of the State, but who appreciate the difficulties in the way of direct confiscation, that by spreading the process over a sufficient number of years and pursuing it after a certain fashion bearing all the outward appearances of a purchase, the expropriation could be effected without the consequences and attendant difficulties of direct confiscation. In other words, there is an impression that the State could "buy-out" the Capitalist class without their knowing it, and that in a sort of painless way this class can be slowly conjured out of existence.

The impression is held in a confused fashion by most of those who cherish it, and will not bear a clear analysis. It is impossible by any jugglery to "buy-out" the universality of the means of production without confiscation.

To prove this, consider a concrete case which puts the problem in the simplest terms:—

A community of twenty-two families lives upon the produce of two farms, the property of only two families out of that twenty-two.

The remaining twenty families are Proletarian. The two families, with their ploughs, stores, land, etc., are Capitalist.

The labour of the twenty proletarian families applied to the land and capital of these two capitalist families produces 300 measures of wheat, of which 200 measures, or 10 measures each, form the annual support of the twenty proletarian families; the remaining 100 measures are the surplus value retained as rent, interest, and profit by the two Capitalist families, each of which has thus a yearly income of 50 measures.

The State proposes to produce, after a certain length of time, a condition of affairs such that the surplus values shall no longer go to the two Capitalist families, but shall be distributed to the advantage of the whole community, while it, the State, shall itself become the unembarrassed owner of both farms.

Now capital is accumulated with the object of a certain return as the reward of accumulation. Instead of spending his money, a man saves it with the object of retaining as the result of that saving a certain yearly revenue. The measure of this does not fall in a particular society at a particular time below a certain level. In other words, if a man cannot get a certain minimum reward for his accumulation, he will not accumulate but spend.

What is called in economics "The Law of Diminishing Returns" acts so that continual additions to capital, other things being equal (that is, the methods of production remaining the same), do not provide a corresponding increase of revenue. A thousand measures of capital applied to a particular area of natural forces will produce, for instance, 40 measures yearly, or 4 per cent.; but 2000 measures applied in the same fashion will not produce 80 measures. They will produce more than the thousand measures did, but not more in proportion; not double. They will produce, say, 60 measures, or 3 per cent., upon the capital. The action of this universal principle automatically checks the accumulation of capital when it has reached such a point that the proportionate return is the least which a man will accept. If it falls below that he will spend rather than accumulate. The limit of this minimum in any particular society at any particular time gives the measure to what we call "*the Effective Desire of Accumulation.*" Thus in England to-day it is a little over 3 per cent. The minimum which limits the accumulation of capital is a minimum return of about one-thirtieth yearly upon such capital, and this we may call for shortness the "E.D.A." of our society at the present time.

When, therefore, the Capitalist estimates the full value of his possessions, he counts them in "so many years' purchase."* And that means that he is willing to take in a lump sum down for his possessions so many times the yearly revenue which he at present enjoys. If his E.D.A. is one-thirtieth, he will take a lump sum representing thirty times his annual revenue.

So far so good. Let us suppose the two Capitalists in our example to have an E.D.A. of one-thirtieth. They will sell to the State if the State can put up 3000 measures of wheat.

Now, of course, the State can do nothing of the

* By an illusion which clever statesmanship could use to the advantage of the community, he even estimates the natural forces he controls (which need no accumulation, but are always present) on the analogy of his capital, and will part with them at "so many years' purchase." It is by taking advantage of this illusion that land purchase schemes (as in Ireland) happily work to the advantage of the dispossessed.

kind. The accumulations of wheat being already in the hands of the Capitalists, and those accumulations amounting to much less than 3000 measures of wheat, the thing appears to be a deadlock.

But it is not a deadlock if the Capitalist is a fool. The State can go to the Capitalists and say: "Hand me over your farms, and against them I will give you guarantee that you shall be paid *rather more than* 100 measures of wheat a year for the thirty years. In fact, I will pay you half as much again until these extra payments amount to a purchase of your original stock."

Out of what does this extra amount come? Out of the State's power to tax.

The State can levy a tax upon the profits of both Capitalists A and B, and pay them the extra with their own money.

In so simple an example it is evident that this "ringing of the changes" would be spotted by the victims, and that they would bring against it precisely the same forces which they would bring against the much simpler and more straightforward process of immediate confiscation.

But it is argued that in a complex State, where you are dealing with myriads of individual Capitalists and thousands of particular forms of profit, the process can be masked.

There are two ways in which the State can mask its

action (according to this policy). It can buy out first one small area of land and capital out of the general taxation and then another, and then another, until the whole has been transferred; or it can tax with peculiar severity certain trades which the rest who are left immune will abandon to their ruin, and with the general taxation plus this special taxation buy out those unfortunate trades which will, of course, have sunk heavily in value under the attack.

The second of these tricks will soon be apparent in any society, however complex; for after one unpopular trade had been selected for attack the trying on of the same methods in another less unpopular field will at once rouse suspicion.*

The first method, however, might have some chance of success, at least for a long time after it was begun, in a highly complex and numerous society were it not for a certain check which comes in of itself. That check is the fact that the Capitalist only takes *more than* his old yearly revenue with the object of reinvesting the surplus.

I have a thousand pounds in Brighton railway stock, yielding me 3 per cent.: £30 a year. The Government asks me to exchange my bit of paper against another bit of paper guaranteeing the payment of £50 a year, that is, an extra rate a year, for so many years as will represent

* Thus you can raid the brewers in a society half-Puritan where brewing is thought immoral by many, but proceed to railway stock and it will be a very different matter.

over and above the regular interest paid a purchase of my stock. The Government's bit of paper promises to pay to the holder £50 a year for, say, thirty-eight years. I am delighted to make the exchange, not because I am such a fool as to enjoy the prospect of my property being extinguished at the end of thirty-eight years, but because I hope to be able to reinvest the extra 20 every year in something else that will bring me in 3 per cent. Thus, at the end of the thirty-eight years I shall (or my heirs) be better off than I was at the beginning of the transaction, and I shall have enjoyed during its maturing my old £30 a year all the same.

The State can purchase thus on a small scale by subsidising purchase out of the general taxation. It can, therefore, play this trick over a small area and for a short time with success. But the moment this area passes a very narrow limit the "market for investment" is found to be restricted, Capital automatically takes alarm, the State can no longer offer its paper guarantees save at an enhanced price. If it tries to turn the position by further raising taxation to what Capital regards as "confiscatory" rates, there will be opposed to its action just the same forces as would be opposed to frank and open expropriation.

The matter is one of plain arithmetic, and all the confusion introduced by the complex mechanism of "finance" can no more change the fundamental and arithmetical principles involved than can the accumulation of triangles in an ordnance survey reduce the internal angles of the largest triangle to less than 180 degrees.[†] In fine: *if you desire to confiscate, you must confiscate.*

You cannot outflank the enemy, as Financiers in the city and sharpers on the race-course outflank the simpler of mankind, nor can you conduct the general process of expropriation upon a muddle-headed hope that somehow or other something will come out of nothing in the end.

There are, indeed, two ways in which the State could exropriate without meeting the resistance that must be present against any attempt at confiscation. But the first of these ways is precarious, the second insufficient.

They are as follows:—

(*1*) The State can promise the Capitalist a larger yearly revenue than he is getting in the expectation that it, the State, can manage the business better than the Capitalist, or that some future expansion will come to its aid. In other words, if the State makes a bigger profit out of the thing than the Capitalist, it can buy out the Capitalist just as a private individual with a similar business proposition can buy him out.

But the converse of this is that if the State has calculated badly, or has bad luck, it would find itself endowing the Capitalists of the future instead of gradually extinguishing them.

---

* In using this metaphor I at once record my apologies to those who believe in elliptical and hyperbolic universes, and confess myself an old-fashioned parabolist. Further, I admit that the triangles in question are spherical.

In this fashion the State could have "socialised" without confiscation the railways of this country if it had taken them over fifty years ago, promising the then owners more than they were then obtaining. But if it had socialised the hansom cab in the nineties, it would now be supporting in perpetuity that worthy but extinct type the cab-owner (and his children for ever) at the expense of the community.

The second way in which the State can expropriate without confiscation is by annuity. It can say to such Capitalists as have no heirs or care little for their fate if they have: "You have only got so much time to live and to enjoy your 30, will you take £50 until you die?" Upon the bargain being accepted the State will, in process of time, though not immediately upon the death of the annuitant, become an unembarrassed owner of what had been the annuitant's share in the means of production. But the area over which this method can be exercised is a very small one. It is not of itself a sufficient instrument for the expropriation of any considerable field.

I need hardly add that as a matter of fact the so-called "Socialist" and confiscatory measures of our time have nothing to do with the problem here discussed. The State is indeed confiscating, that is, it is taxing in many cases in such a fashion as to impoverish the tax-payer and is lessening his capital rather than shearing his income. But it is not putting the proceeds into the means of production. It is either using them for immediate consumption in the shape of new official salaries or handing them over to another set of Capitalists.

But these practical considerations of the way in which sham Socialist experiments are working belong rather to my next section, in which I shall deal with the actual beginnings of the Servile State in our midst.

---

* Thus the money levied upon the death of some not very wealthy squire and represented by, say, locomotives in the Argentine, turns into two miles of palings for the pleasant back gardens of a thousand new officials under the Inebriates Bill, or is simply handed over to the shareholders of the Prudential under the Insurance Act. In the first case the locomotives have been given back to the Argentine, and after a long series of exchanges have been bartered against a great number of wood-palings from the Baltic not exactly reproductive wealth. In the second case the locomotives which used to be the squire's hands become, or their equivalent becomes, means of production in the hands of the Sassoons.

SECTION NINE

THE SERVILE STATE HAS BEGUN

SECTION THE NINTH
THE SERVILE STATE HAS BEGUN

In this last division of my book I deal with the actual appearance of the Servile State in certain laws and proposals now familiar to the Industrial Society of modern England. These are the patent objects, "laws and projects of laws," which lend stuff to my argument, and show that it is based not upon a mere deduction, but upon an observation of things.

Two forms of this proof are evident: first, the laws and proposals which subject the *Proletariat* to Servile conditions; next, the fact that the *Capitalist*, so far from being expropriated by modern "Socialist" experiments, is being confirmed in his power.

I take these in their order, and I begin by asking in what statutes or proposals the Servile State first appeared among us.

A false conception of our subject might lead one to find the origins of the Servile State in the restrictions imposed upon certain forms of manufacture, and the corresponding duties laid upon the Capitalist in the interest of his workmen. The Factory Laws, as they are in this country, would seem to offer upon this superficial and erroneous view a starting point. They do nothing of the kind; and the view *is* superficial and erroneous because it neglects the fundamentals of the case. What distinguishes the Servile State is not the interference of law with the action of any citizen even in connection with industrial matters. Such interference may or may not indicate the presence of a Servile status. It in no way indicates the presence of that status when it forbids a particular kind of human action to be undertaken by the citizen as a citizen.

The legislator says, for instance, "You may pluck roses; but as I notice that you sometimes scratch yourself, I will put you in prison unless you cut them with scissors at least 122 millimetres long, and I will appoint one thousand inspectors to go round the country seeing whether the law is observed. My brother-in-law shall be at the head of the Department at £2000 a year."

We are all familiar with that type of legislation. We are all familiar with the arguments for and against it in any particular case. We may regard it as onerous, futile, or beneficent, or in any other light, according to our various temperaments. But it does not fall within the category of servile legislation, because it establishes no distinction between two classes of citizens, marking off the one as legally distinct from the other by a criterion of manual labour or of income.

This is even true of such regulations as those which compel a Cotton Mill, for instance, to have no less than such and such an amount of cubic space for each operative, and such and such protection for dangerous machinery. These laws do not concern themselves with the nature, the amount, or even the existence of a contract for service. The object, for example, of the law which compels one to fence off certain types of machinery is simply to protect human life, regardless of whether the human being so protected is rich or poor, Capitalist or Proletarian. These laws may in effect work in our society so that the Capitalist is made responsible for the Proletarian, but he is not responsible *quâ* Capitalist, nor is the Proletarian protected *quâ* Proletarian.

In the same way the law may compel me, if I am a Riparian owner, to put up a fence of statutory strength wherever the water of my river is of more than a statutory depth. Now it cannot compel me to do this unless I am the owner of the land. In a sense, therefore, this might be called the recognition of my Status, because, by the nature of the case, only landowners can be affected by the law, and landowners would be compelled by it to safeguard the lives of all, whether they were or were not owners of land.

But the category so established would be purely accidental. The object and method of the law do not concern themselves with a distinction between citizens.

A close observer might indeed discover certain points in the Factory laws, details and phrases, which did distinctly connote the existence of a Capitalist and of a Proletarian class. But we must take the statutes as a whole and the order in which they were produced, above all, the general motive and expressions governing each main statute, in order to judge whether such examples of interference give us an origin or not.

The verdict will be that they do not. Such legislation may be oppressive in any degree or necessary in any degree, but it does not establish status in the place of contract, and it is not, therefore, servile.

Neither are those laws servile which in practice attach to the poor and not to the rich. Compulsory education is in legal theory required of every citizen for his children. The state of mind which goes with plutocracy exempts of course all above a certain standard of wealth from this law. But the law does apply to the universality of the commonwealth, and all families resident in Great Britain (not in Ireland) are subject to its provisions.

These are not origins. A true origin to the legislation I approach comes later. The first example of servile legislation to be discovered upon the Statute Book is that which establishes the present form of *Employer's Liability*.

I am far from saying that that law was passed, as modern laws are beginning to be passed, with the direct object of establishing a new status; though it was passed with some consciousness on the part of the legislator that such a new status was in existence as a social fact. Its motive was merely humane, and the relief which it afforded seemed merely necessary at the time; but it is an instructive example of the way in which a small neglect of strict doctrine and a slight toleration of anomaly admit great changes into the State.

There had existed from all time in every community, and there was founded upon common sense, the legal doctrine that if one citizen was so placed with regard to another by contract that he must in the fulfilment of that contract perform certain services, and if those services accidentally involved damages to a third party, not the actual perpetrator of the damage, but he who designed the particular operation leading to it was responsible.

The point is subtle, but, as I say, fundamental. It involved no distinction of status between employer and employed.

Citizen A offered citizen B a sack of wheat down if citizen B would plough for him a piece of land which might or might not produce more than a sack of wheat.

Of course citizen A expected it would produce more, and was awaiting a surplus value, or he would not have made the contract with citizen B. But, at any rate, citizen B put his name to the agreement, and as a free man, capable of contracting, was correspondingly bound to fulfil it.

In fulfilling this contract the ploughshare B is driving destroys a pipe conveying water by agreement through A's land to C. C suffers damage, and to recover the equivalent of that damage his action in justice and common sense can only be against A, for B was carrying out a plan and instruction of which A was the author. C is a third party who had nothing to do with such a contract and could not possibly have justice save by his chances of getting it from A, who was the true author of the unintentional loss inflicted, since he designed the course of work.

But when the damage is not done to C at all, but to B, who is concerned with a work the risks of which are known and willingly undertaken, it is quite another matter.

Citizen A contracts with citizen B that citizen B, in consideration of a sack of wheat, shall plough a bit of land. Certain known risks must attach to that operation. Citizen B, if he is a free man, undertakes those risks with his eyes open. For instance, he may sprain his wrist in turning the plough, or one of the horses may kick him while he is having his bread-and-cheese. If upon such an accident A is compelled to pay damages to B, a difference of status is at once recognised. B undertook to do work which, by all the theory of free contract, was, with its risks and its expense of energy, the equivalent in B's own eyes of a sack of wheat; yet a law is passed to say that B can have more than that sack of wheat if he is hurt.

There is no converse right of A against B. If the employer suffers by such an accident to the employee, he is not allowed to dock that sack of wheat, though it was regarded in the contract as the equivalent to a certain amount of labour to be performed which, as a fact, has not been performed. A has no action unless B has been *culpably* negligent or remiss. In other words, the mere fact that one man is *working* and the other not is the fundamental consideration on which the law is built, and the law says: "You are not a free man making a free contract with all its consequences. You are a worker, and therefore an inferior: you are an *employee*; and that *status* gives you a special position which would not be recognised in the other party to the contract."

The principle is pushed still further when an employer is made liable for an accident happening to one of his employees at the hands of another employee.

A gives a sack of wheat to B and D each if they will dig a well for him. All three parties are cognisant of the risks and accept them in the contract. B, holding the rope on which D is lowered, lets it slip. If they were all three men of exactly equal status, obviously D's action would be against B. But they are not of equal status in England to-day. B and D are *employees*, and are therefore in a special and inferior position before the law compared with their employer A. D's action is, by this novel principle, no longer against B, who accidentally injured him by a personal act, however involuntary, for which a free man would be responsible, but against A, who was innocent of the whole business.

Now in all this it is quite clear that A has peculiar duties not because he is a citizen, but because he is something more: an employer; and B and D have special claims on A, not because they are citizens, but because they are something less: *viz. employees.* They can *claim protection* from A, as inferiors of a superior in a State admitting such distinctions and patronage.

It will occur at once to the reader that in our existing social state the employee will be very grateful for such legislation. One workman cannot recover from another simply because the other will have no goods out of which to pay damages. Let the burden, therefore, fall upon the rich man!

Excellent. But that is not the point. To argue thus is to say that Servile legislation is necessary if we are to solve the problems raised by Capitalism. It remains servile legislation none the less. It is legislation that would not exist in a society where property was well divided and where a citizen could normally pay damages for the harm he had himself caused.*

This first trickle of the stream, however, though it is of considerable historical interest as a point of departure, is not of very definite moment to our subject compared with the great bulk of later proposals, some of which are already law, others upon the point of becoming law, and which definitely recognise the Servile State, the re-establishment of status in the place of contract, and the universal division of citizens into two categories of employers and employed.

These last merit a very different consideration, for they will represent to history the conscious and designed entry of Servile Institutions into the old Christian State.

---

* How true it is that the idea of status underlies this legislation can easily be tested by taking parallel cases, in one of which working men are concerned, in the other the professional class. If I contract to write for a publisher a complete History of the County of Rutland, and in the pursuit of that task, while examining some object of historical interest, fall down a pit, I should not be able to recover against the publisher. But if I dress in mean clothes, and the same publisher, deceived, gives me a month's work at cleaning out his ornamental water and I am wounded in that occupation by a fierce fish, he will be mulcted to my advantage, and that roundly.

They are not "origins," small indications of coming change which the historian will painfully discover as a curiosity. They are the admitted foundations of a new order, deliberately planned by a few, confusedly accepted by the many, as the basis upon which a novel and stable society shall arise to replace the unstable and passing phase of Capitalism.

They fall roughly into three categories:—

(1) Measures by which the insecurity of the proletariat shall be relieved through the action of the employing class, or of the proletariat itself acting under compulsion.

(2) Measures by which the employer shall be compelled to give not less than a certain minimum for any labour he may purchase, and

(3) Measures which compel a man lacking the means of production to labour, though he may have made no contract to that effect.

The last two, as will be seen in a moment, are complementary one of another.

As to the first: Measures to palliate the insecurity of the proletariat.

We have of this an example in actual law at this moment. And that law—the Insurance Act—(whose political source and motive I am not here discussing) follows in every particular the lines of a Servile State.

(*a*) Its fundamental criterion is employment. In other words, I am compelled to enter a scheme providing me against the mischances of illness and unemployment not because I am a citizen, but only if I am:

(1) Exchanging services for goods; and either

(2) Obtaining less than a certain amount of goods for those services, or

(3) A vulgar fellow working with his hands. The law carefully excludes from its provisions those forms of labour to which the educated and therefore powerful classes are subject, and further excludes from compulsion the mass of those who are for the moment earning enough to make them a class to be reckoned with as economically free. I may be a writer of books who, should he fall ill, will leave in the greatest distress the family which he supports. If the legislator were concerned for the morals of citizens, I should most undoubtedly come under this law, under the form of a compulsory insurance added to my income tax. But the legislator is not concerned with people of my sort. He is concerned with a new status which he recognises in the State, to wit, the proletariat. He envisages the proletariat not quite accurately as men either poor, or, if they are not poor, at any rate vulgar people working with their hands, and he legislates accordingly.

(*b*) Still more striking, as an example of status taking the place of contract, is the fact that this law puts the duty of controlling the proletariat and of seeing that the law is obeyed not upon the proletariat itself, but upon the *Capitalist class.*

Now this point is of an importance that cannot be exaggerated.

The future historian, whatever his interest in the first indications of that profound revolution through which we are so rapidly passing, will most certainly fix upon that one point as the cardinal landmark of our times. The legislator surveying the Capitalist State proposes as a remedy for certain of its evils the establishment of two categories in the State, compels the lower man to registration, to a tax, and the rest of it, and further compels the upper man to be the instrument in enforcing that registration and in collecting that tax. No one acquainted with the way in which any one of the great changes of the past has taken place, the substitution of tenure for the Roman proprietary right in land. Or the substitution of the mediaeval peasant for the serf of the Dark Ages, can possibly misunderstand the significance of such a turning point in our history.

Whether it will be completed or whether a reaction will destroy it is another matter. Its mere proposal is of the greatest possible moment in the inquiry we are here pursuing.

Of the next two groups, the fixing of a Minimum Wage and the Compulsion to Labour (which, as I have said, and will shortly show, are complementary one to the other), neither has yet appeared in actual legislation, but both are planned, both thought out, both possessed of powerful advocates, and both upon the threshold of positive law.

The fixing of a Minimum Wage, with a definite sum fixed by statute, has not yet entered our laws, but the first step towards such a consummation has been taken in the shape of giving legal sanction to some hypothetical Minimum Wage which shall be arrived at after discussion within a particular trade. That trade is, of course, the mining industry. The law does not say: "No Capitalist shall pay a miner less than so many shillings for so many hours' work." But it does say: "Figures having been arrived at by local boards, any miner working within the area of each board can claim by force of law the minimum sum established by such boards." It is evident that from this step to the next, which shall define some sliding scale of remuneration for labour according to prices and the profits of capital, is an easy and natural transition. It would give both parties what each immediately requires: to capital a guarantee against disturbance; to labour sufficiency and security. The whole thing is an excellent object lesson in little of that general movement from free contract to status, and from the Capitalist to the Servile State, which is the tide of our time.

The neglect of older principles as abstract and doctrinaire; the immediate need of both parties immediately satisfied; the unforeseen but necessary consequence of satisfying such needs in such a fashion all these, which are apparent in the settlement the mining industry has begun, are the typical forces producing the

Servile State.

Consider in its largest aspect the nature of such a settlement.
The Proletarian accepts a position in which he produces for the Capitalist a certain total of economic values, and retains out of that total a portion only, leaving to the Capitalist all surplus value. The Capitalist, on his side, is guaranteed in the secure and permanent expectation of that surplus value through all the perils of social envy; the Proletarian is guaranteed in a sufficiency and a security for that sufficiency; but by the very action of such a guarantee there is withdrawn from him the power to refuse his labour and thus to aim at putting himself in possession of the means of production.

Such schemes definitely divide citizens into two classes, the Capitalist and the Proletarian. They make it impossible for the second to combat the privileged position of the first. They introduce into the positive laws of the community a recognition of social facts which already divide Englishmen into two groups of economically more free and economically less free, and they stamp with the authority of the State a new constitution of society. Society is recognised as no longer consisting of free men bargaining freely for their labour or any other commodity in their possession, but of two contrasting status, owners and non-owners. The first must not be allowed to leave the second without subsistence; the second must not be allowed to obtain that grip upon the means of production which is the privilege of the first. It is true that this first experiment is small in degree and tentative in quality; but to judge the movement as a general whole we must not only consider the expression it has actually received so far in positive law, but the mood of our time.

When this first experiment in a minimum wage was being debated in Parliament, what was the great issue of debate? Upon what did those who were the most ardent reformers particularly insist? *Not* that the miners should have an avenue open to them for obtaining possession of the mines; not even that the State should have an avenue open to it for obtaining such possession; *but that the minimum wage should be fixed at a certain satisfactory level!* That, as our recent experience testifies for all of us, was the crux of the quarrel. And that such a point should be the crux, not the socialisation of the mines, nor the admission of the proletariat to the means of production, but only a sufficiency and a security of wage, is amply significant of the perhaps irresistible forces which are making in the direction for which I argue in this book.

There was here no attempt of the Capitalist to impose Servile conditions nor of the Proletarian to resist them. Both parties were agreed upon that fundamental change. The discussion turned upon the minimum limit of subsistence to be securely provided, a point which left aside, because it took for granted, the establishment of *some* minimum in any case.

Next, let it be noted (for it is of moment to a later part of my argument) that experiments of this sort promise to extend piecemeal. There is no likelihood, judging by men's actions and speech, of some grand general scheme for the establishment of a minimum wage throughout the community. Such a scheme would, of course, be as truly an establishment of the Servile State as piecemeal schemes. But, as we shall see in a moment, the extension of the principle piecemeal has a considerable effect upon the forms which compulsion may take.

The miners' refusal to work, with the exaggerated panic it caused, bred this first tentative appearance of the minimum wage in our laws. Normally, capital prefers free labour with its margin of destitution; for such an anarchy, ephemeral though it is of its nature, while it lasts provides cheap labour; from the narrowest point of view it provides in the still competitive areas of Capitalism a better chance for profits.

But as one group of workmen after another, concerned with trades immediately necessary to the life of the nation, and therefore tolerating but little interruption, learn the power which combination gives them, it is inevitable that the legislator (concentrated as he is upon momentary remedies for difficulties as they arise) should propose for one such trade after another the remedy of a minimum wage.

There can be little doubt that, trade by trade, the principle will extend. For instance, the two and a half millions now guaranteed against unemployment are guaranteed against it for a certain weekly sum. That weekly sum must bear some relation to their estimated earnings when they are in employment.

It is a short step from the calculation of

unemployment benefit (its being fixed by statute at a certain level, and that level determined by something which is regarded as the just remuneration of labour in that trade); it is a short step, I say, from that to a statutory fixing of the sums paid during employment.

The State says to the Serf: "I saw to it that you should have so much when you were unemployed. I find that in some rare cases my arrangement leads to your getting more when you are unemployed than when you are employed. I further find that in many cases, though you get more when you are employed, yet the difference is not sufficient to tempt a lazy man to work, or to make him take any particular trouble to get work. I must see to this."

The provision of a fixed schedule during unemployment thus inevitably leads to the examination, the defining, and at last the imposition of a minimum wage during employment; and every compulsory provision for unemployed benefits is the seed of a minimum wage.

Of still greater effect is the mere presence of State regulation in such a matter. The fact that the State has begun to gather statistics of wages over these large areas of industry, and to do so not for a mere statistical object, but a practical one, and the fact that the State has begun to immix the action of positive law and constraint with the older system of free bargaining, mean that the whole weight of its influence is now in favour of regulation. It is no rash prophecy to assert that in the near future our industrial society will see a gradually extending area of industry in which from two sides the fixing of wages by statute shall appear. From the one side it will come in the form of the State examining the conditions of labour in connection with its own schemes for establishing sufficiency and security by insurance. From the other side it will come through the reasonable proposals to make contracts between groups of labour and groups of capital enforceable in the Courts.

So much, then, for the Principle of a Minimum Wage. It has already appeared in our laws. It is certain to spread. But how does the presence of this introduction of a Minimum form part of the advance towards the Servile State?

I have said that the principle of a minimum wage involves as its converse the principle of compulsory labour. Indeed, most of the importance which the principle of a minimum wage has for this inquiry lies in that converse necessity of compulsory labour which it involves.

But as the connection between the two may not be clear at first sight, we must do more than take it for granted. We must establish it by process of reason.

There are two distinct forms in which the whole policy of enforcing security and sufficiency by law for the proletariat produce a corresponding policy of compulsory labour.

The first of these forms is the compulsion which the Courts will exercise upon either of the parties concerned in the giving and in the receiving of the minimum wage. The second form is the necessity under which society will find itself, when once the principle of the minimum wage is conceded, coupled with the principle of sufficiency and security, to maintain those whom the minimum wage excludes from the area of normal employment.

As to the first form:—

A Proletarian group has struck a bargain with a group of Capitalists to the effect that it will produce for that capital ten measures of value in a year, will be content to receive six measures of value for itself, and will leave four measures as surplus value for the Capitalists. The bargain is ratified; the Courts have the power to enforce it. If the Capitalists by some trick of fines or by bluntly breaking their word pay out in wages less than the six measures, the Courts must have some power of constraining them. In other words, there must be some sanction to the action of the law. There must be some power of punishment, and, through punishment, of compulsion. Conversely, if the men, having struck this bargain, go back upon their word; if individuals among them or sections among them cease work with a new demand for seven measures instead of six, the Courts must have the power of constraining and of punishing them. Where the bargain is ephemeral or at any rate extended over only reasonable limits of time, it would be straining language perhaps to say that each individual case of constraint exercised against the workmen would be a case of compulsory labour. But extend the system over a long period of years, make it

normal to industry and accepted as a habit in men's daily conception of the way in which their lives should be conducted, and the method is necessarily transformed into a system of compulsory labour. In trades where wages fluctuate little this will obviously be the case. "You, the agricultural labourers of this district, have taken fifteen shillings a week for a very long time.
It has worked perfectly well. There seems no reason why you should have more. Nay, you put your hands to it through your officials in the year so and so that you regarded that sum as sufficient. Such and such of your members are now refusing to perform what this Court regards as a contract. They must return within the limits of that contract or suffer the consequences."

Remember what power analogy exercises over men's minds, and how, when systems of the sort are common to many trades, they will tend to create a general point of view for all trades. Remember also how comparatively slight a threat is already sufficient to control men in our industrial society, the proletarian mass of which is accustomed to live from week to week under peril of discharge, and has grown readily amenable to the threat of any reduction in those wages upon which it can but just subsist.

Nor are the Courts enforcing such contracts or quasi-contracts (as they will come to be regarded) the only inducement.

A man has been compelled by law to put aside sums from his wages as insurance against unemployment. But he is no longer the judge of how such sums shall be used. They are not in his possession; they are not even in the hands of some society which he can really control. They are in the hands of a Government official. "Here is work offered you at twenty-five shillings a week. If you do not take it you certainly shall not have a right to the money you have been compelled to put aside. If you will take it the sum shall still stand to your credit, and when next in my judgment your unemployment is not due to your recalcitrance and refusal to labour, I will permit you to have some of your money: not otherwise." Dovetailing in with this machinery of compulsion is all that mass of registration and docketing which is accumulating through the use of Labour Exchanges. Not only will the Official have the power to enforce special contracts, or the power to coerce individual men to labour under the threat of a fine, but he will also have a series of *dossiers* by which the record of each workman can be established. No man, once so registered and known, can escape; and, of the nature of the system, the numbers caught in the net must steadily increase until the whole mass of labour is mapped out and controlled.

These are very powerful instruments of compulsion indeed. They already exist. They are already a part of our laws.

Lastly, there is the obvious bludgeon of "compulsory arbitration": a bludgeon so obvious that it is revolting even to our proletariat. Indeed, I know of no civilised European state which has succumbed to so gross a suggestion. For it is a frank admission of servitude at one step, and for good and all, such as men of our culture are not yet prepared to swallow.

So much, then, for the first argument and the first form in which compulsory labour is seen to be a direct and necessary consequence of establishing a minimum wage and of scheduling employment to a scale.

The second is equally clear. In the production of wheat the healthy and skilled man who can produce ten measures of wheat is compelled to work for six measures, and the Capitalist is compelled to remain content with four measures for his share. The law will punish him if he tries to get out of his legal obligation and to pay his workmen less than six measures of wheat during the year. What of the man who is not sufficiently strong or skilled to produce even six measures? Will the Capitalist be constrained to pay him more than the values he can produce? Most certainly not. The whole structure of production as it was erected during the Capitalist phase of our industry has been left intact by the new laws and customs. Profit is still left a necessity. If it were destroyed, still more if a loss were imposed by law, that would be a contradiction of the whole spirit in which all these reforms are being undertaken. They are being undertaken with the object of establishing stability where there is now instability, and of "reconciling," as the ironic phrase goes, "the interests of capital and labour." It would be impossible, without a general ruin,

---

* But it has twice been brought forward in due process as a Bill in Parliament!

to compel capital to lose upon the man who is not worth even the minimum wage. How shall that element of insecurity and instability be eliminated? To support the man gratuitously because he cannot earn a minimum wage, when all the rest of the commonwealth is working for its guaranteed wages, is to put a premium upon incapacity and sloth. The man must be made to work. He must be taught, if possible, to produce those economic values, which are regarded as the minimum of sufficiency. He must be kept at that work even if he cannot produce the minimum, lest his presence as a free labourer should imperil the whole scheme of the minimum wage, and introduce at the same time a continuous element of instability. Hence he is necessarily a subject for forced labour. We have not yet in this country, established by force of law, the right to this form of compulsion, but it is an inevitable consequence of those other reforms which have just been reviewed. The "Labour Colony" (a prison so called because euphemism is necessary to every transition) will be erected to absorb this surplus, and that last form of compulsion will crown the edifice of these reforms. They will then be complete so far as the subject classes are concerned, and even though this particular institution of the "Labour Colony " (logically the last of all) precede in time other forms of compulsion, it will make the advent of those other forms of compulsion more certain, facile, and rapid.

There remains one last remark to be made upon the concrete side of my subject. I have in this last section illustrated the tendency towards the Servile State from actual laws and actual projects with which all are to-day familiar in English industrial society, and I have shown how these are certainly establishing the proletariat in a novel, but to them satisfactory, Servile Status.

It remains to point out in a very few lines the complementary truth that what should be the very essence of Collectivist Reform, to wit, the translation of the means of production from the hands of private owners to the hands of public officials, is nowhere being attempted. So far from its being attempted, all so-called "Socialistic" experiments in municipalisation and nationalisation are merely increasing the dependence of the community upon the Capitalist class. To prove this, we need only observe that every single one of these experiments is effected by a loan.

Now what is meant in economic reality by these municipal loans and national loans raised for the purpose of purchasing certain small sections of the means of production?

Certain Capitalists own a number of rails, cars, etc. They put to work upon these certain Proletarians, and the result is a certain total of economic values. Let the surplus values obtainable by the Capitalists after the subsistence of the proletarians is provided for amount to £10,000 a year. We all know how a system of this sort is "Municipalised. A "loan" is raised. It bears "interest." It is saddled with a "sinking fund."

Now this loan is not really made in money, though the terms of it are in money. It is, at the end of a long string of exchanges, nothing more nor less than the loan of the cars, the rails, etc., by the Capitalists to the Municipality. And the Capitalists require, before they will strike the bargain, a guarantee that the whole of their old profit shall be paid to them, together with a further yearly sum, which after a certain number of years shall represent the original value of the concern when they handed it over. These last additional sums are called the "sinking fund"; the, continued payment of the old surplus values is called the "interest."

In theory certain small sections of the means of production might be acquired in this way. That particular section would have been "socialised." The "Sinking Fund" (that is, the paying of the Capitalists for their plant by instalments) might be met out of the general taxation imposed on the community, considering how large that is compared with any one experiment of the kind. The "interest" may by good management be met out of the true profits of the tramways. At the end of a certain number of years the community will be in possession of the tramways, will no longer be exploited in this particular by Capitalism, will have bought out Capitalism from the general taxes, and, in so far as the purchase money paid has been consumed and not saved or invested by the Capitalists, a small measure of "socialisation" will have been achieved.

As a fact things are never so favourable.

In practice three conditions militate against even these tiny experiments in expropriation: the fact that the implements are always sold at much more than their true value; the fact that the purchase includes non-productive things; and the fact that the rate of borrowing is much faster than the rate of repayment. These three adverse conditions lead in practice to nothing but the riveting of Capitalism more securely round the body of the State.

For what is it that is paid for when a tramway, for instance, is taken over? Is it the true capital alone, the actual plant, which is paid for, even at an exaggerated price? Far from it! Over and above the rails and the cars, there are all the commissions that have been made, all the champagne luncheons, all the lawyers' fees, all the compensations to this man and to that man, all the bribes. Nor does this exhaust the argument. Tramways represent a productive investment. What about pleasure gardens, wash-houses, baths, libraries, monuments, and the rest? The greater part of these things are the product of "loans." When you put up a public institution you borrow the bricks and the mortar and the iron and the wood and the tiles from Capitalists, *and you pledge yourself to pay interest, and to produce a sinking fund precisely as though a town hall or a bath were a piece of reproductive machinery.*

To this must be added the fact that a considerable proportion of the purchases are failures: purchases of things just before they are driven out by some new invention; while on the top of the whole business you have the fact that the borrowing goes on at a far greater rate than the repayment.

In a word, all these experiments up and down Europe during our generation, municipal and national, have resulted in an indebtedness to capital increasing rather more than twice, but not three times, as fast as the rate of repayment. The interest which capital demands with a complete indifference as to whether the loan is productive or non-productive amounts to rather more than 1 $^1/_2$ per cent, excess over the produce of the various experiments, even though we count in the most lucrative and successful of these, such as the state railways of many countries, and the thoroughly successful municipal enterprises of many modern towns.

Capitalism has seen to it that it shall be a winner and not a loser by this form of sham Socialism, as by every other. And the same forces which in practice forbid confiscation see to it that the attempt to mask confiscation by purchase shall not only fail, but shall turn against those who have not had the courage to make a frontal attack upon privilege.

With these concrete examples showing how Collectivism, in attempting its practice, does but confirm the Capitalist position, and showing how our laws have already begun to impose a Servile Status upon the Proletariat, I end the argumentative thesis of this book.

I believe I have proved my case.

The future of industrial society, and in particular of English society, left to its own direction, is a future in which subsistence and security shall be guaranteed for the Proletariat, but shall be guaranteed at the expense of the old political freedom and by the establishment of that Proletariat in a status really, though not nominally, servile. At the same time, the Owners will be guaranteed in their profits, the whole machinery of production in the smoothness of its working, and that stability which has been lost under the Capitalist phase of society will be found once more.

The internal strains which have threatened society during its Capitalist phase will be relaxed and eliminated, and the community will settle down upon that Servile basis which was its foundation before the advent of the Christian faith, from which that faith slowly weaned it, and to which in the decay of that faith it naturally returns.

CONCLUSION

CONCLUSION

It is possible to portray a great social movement of the past with accuracy and in detail if one can spare to the task the time necessary for research and further bring to it a certain power of co-ordination by which a great mass of detail can be integrated and made one whole.

Such a task is rarely accomplished, but it does not exceed the powers of history.

With regard to the future it is otherwise. No one can say even in its largest aspect or upon its chief structural line what that future will be. He can only present the main tendencies of his time: he can only determine the equation of the curve and presume that that equation will apply more or less to its next developments.

So far as I can judge, those societies which broke with the continuity of Christian civilisation in the sixteenth century—which means, roughly, North Germany and Great Britain tend at present to the re-establishment of a Servile Status. It will be diversified by local accident, modified by local character, hidden under many forms. But it will come.

That the mere Capitalist anarchy cannot endure is patent to all men. That only a very few possible solutions to it exist should be equally patent to all. For my part, as I have said in these pages, I do not believe there are more than two: a reaction towards well-divided property, or the re-establishment of servitude. I cannot believe that theoretical Collectivism, now so plainly failing, will ever inform a real and living society.

But my conviction that the re-establishment of the Servile Status in industrial society is actually upon us does not lead me to any meagre and mechanical prophecy of what the future of Europe shall be. The force of which I have been speaking is not the only force in the field. There is a complex knot of forces underlying any nation once Christian; a smouldering of the old fires.

Moreover, one can point to European societies which will most certainly reject any such solution' of our Capitalist problem, just as the same societies have either rejected, or lived suspicious of, Capitalism itself, and have rejected or lived suspicious of that industrial organisation which till lately identified itself with "progress" and national well-being.

These societies are in the main the same as those which, in that great storm of the sixteenth century,—the capital episode in the story of Christendom—held fast to tradition and saved the continuity of morals. Chief among them should be noted to-day the French and the Irish.

I would record it as an impression and no more that the Servile State, strong as the tide is making for it in Prussia and in England to-day, will be modified, checked, perhaps defeated in war, certainly halted in its attempt to establish itself completely, by the strong reaction which these freer societies upon its flank will perpetually exercise.

Ireland has decided for a free peasantry, and our generation has seen the solid foundation of that institution laid. In France the many experiments which elsewhere have successfully introduced the Servile State have been contemptuously rejected by the populace, and (most significant!) a recent attempt to register and to "insure" the artisans as a separate category of citizens has broken down in the face of an universal and a virile contempt.

That this second factor in the development of the future, the presence of free societies, will destroy the tendency to the Servile State elsewhere I do not affirm, but I believe that it will modify that tendency, certainly by example and perhaps by direct attack. And as I am upon the whole hopeful that the Faith will recover its intimate and guiding place in the heart of Europe, so I believe that this sinking back into our original Paganism (for the tendency to the Servile State is nothing less) will in due time be halted and reversed.

Videat Deus.

SOCIALISM and the SERVILE STATE

A DEBATE

BETWEEN MESSRS.

Hilaire Belloc and
J. Ramsay MacDonald, M.P.

THE SOUTH WEST LONDON FEDERATION OF THE INDEPENDENT LABOUR PARTY. 1911.

EXPLANATORY NOTE.

That the unreality of the Collectivist ideal is apparent from the fact that contemporary Collectivist effort is leading, not to Collectivism, but to the Servile State.

The Debate on the above proposition, of which a Verbatim Report is here given, was held at the Memorial Hall, London, E.G., on Friday, May 5, 1911, under the auspices of the South-West London Federation of the Independent Labour Party. Mr. Hilaire Belloc took the affirmative and Mr. J. Ramsay MacDonald, M.P., the negative. Mr. A. G. Gardiner (Editor of the "Daily News") presided over an audience which packed the Hall; an audience which contained, among its number, people of widely differing opinions about the subject of Debate; an audience which, though keenly interested, was a very orderly one indeed. Neither of the Disputants require any lengthy introduction: Mr. Belloc was (1906-10) Liberal M.P. for South Salford, and is a prominent man of letters; Mr. MacDonald is a well-known member of the I.L.P., has been Secretary to the Labour Party since its inception, and is the present Chairman of its Parliamentary Group. I have only to add that this Report has been approved by both gentlemen.

H.M. May, 1911.

VERBATIM REPORT.

THE CHAIRMAN: Ladies and gentlemen, we are met tonight to hear, I suppose, the oldest debate in the world. When the first man looked out at Creation—I am beginning a little far back, but you need not feel concerned on that account—when the first man looked out on Creation there was one subject that probably filled his mind. That subject was the Mystery of the Universe in which he found himself placed. He saw the glory of the sun by day and the mystery of the stars by night, he saw the pageant of the seasons pass before him, he heard the voice of the thunder-cloud, and saw the sword of the lightning stab the earth, and in the presence of all this splendid spectacle he fashioned his thoughts of God and the omnipotent powers that encompassed him. But when he ceased to dwell alone, he found other things to talk about. He began to discuss his fellowman. He began in a word, a debate on Socialism, and he has been debating it ever since, and he will go on debating it, I fancy, until the last two men, who will probably be a Jew and a Chinaman, sit over the embers of the last fire to catch the latest breath of the expiring atmosphere. For the subject is eternal and inexhaustible. It is at the foundation of the whole history of human society. The history of society is, in the first place, an attempt to discover how we may live decently and comfortably with our fellowmen. We are told to go and learn of the ant. I believe the ants and the bees have solved the problem. They have solved it on a strictly Socialist and Collectivist basis. They recognise nothing and they have nothing but a collective conscience, and any individualist who turned up among them would suffer a very short shrift. Anyone who knows, who is familiar with, a hive will be familiar with those scenes when the workers bundle the drones out on the ground beneath and leave them to crawl about and starve. There is a moral, no doubt, in that, even for human society, but after all men are not ants and bees. They are not instinctive and automatic Socialists or Collectivists. The first and foremost fact about man is that he is an individual, with personal aims and thoughts, and purposes and passions and appetites. He insists on individual liberty. He is, in fact, a solitary individual whose ultimate fastness is never really penetrated by his fellow's. Even in his punishments he is alone. "The sins ye do by two and two are paid for one by one." Well, that being so, he is therefore clearly differentiated from our friends the ants, but at the same time, so ridiculous a creature is he, that while Individualist to begin with, he insists on becoming a social animal. He is gregarious in his habits and interdependent in his nature, and that being so it becomes necessary for him to subordinate his personal aims and his individual will in a very large degree and in a multitude of aspects to the general necessities and the common interests of the society in which he lives. There's the rub. There is the cause of that eternal conflict which has been waged in ail countries and in all ages and will go on being waged until we cease to be. Well now, into this great argument it is fortunately not my duty to enter. I am here simply as a sort of Buffer State between the belligerents. I am a friend of both the Montagues and Capulets. I keep the ring and take care that there are no illegitimate blows struck, and that the victory goes—to whomsoever it goes—as the result of an honourable combat. Neither of the combatants needs any introduction to any English audience. They are known wherever our language is spoken as among the leading and foremost figures intellectually of our time. Just one word I may say as to the procedure. Mr. Belloc will open by speaking to the motion which is in his name, and he will speak for half-an-hour. Then Mr. MacDonald will reply for half-an-hour. Mr. Belloc will have a further twenty minutes, Mr. MacDonald a further twenty minutes; and finally, there will be ten minutes each. I now call upon Mr. Belloc to open.

MR. BELLOC: I am going to ask you, Mr. Chairman, and ladies and gentlemen, with an insufficient voice, to follow so far as I am concerned—and I am sure so far as Mr. MacDonald is concerned, for he is a Scotchman—a certain process of reasoning, and I am going to beg you—I have no need to beg him—to permit the discussion to follow those particular lines which follow from its definition. I am sorry for this, for this is to give pain and not pleasure. I am not here to argue against the Collectivist theory. I am not here to-night to say that I think it is of this or of that general good or evil nature. I am here to defend a particular and positive thesis, and Mr. MacDonald is here to destroy that thesis. I want you to note it very clearly at the beginning of the discussion, not only because that thesis is the object, the material, of what we are dealing with to-night in this particular debate, but because it is, in my opinion at least, by far the most practical matter, by far (I prefer to say) the most immediate and real matter in the politics of Western Europe, to-day. I maintain that the effort of Collectivist idealism and of Collectivist speakers, writers, and thinkers, is having as its result, not as its object, with the material with which it disposes—to wit, human nature, and especially Western European human nature—not the establishment of the Collectivist or Socialist State, nor an approach thereto, but the establishment of what I shall call the Servile State. And I shall begin by defining my terms when I use the words the Servile State. I take it that man—though it is not necessary to my definition: it is necessary to an explanation of my thought—I take it that man demands in the economic sphere two things, which I will call Sufficiency and Security. Let no one pretend that those things need a strict and absolute definition. But each of us, by examining himself, knows at once that not where property is concerned, or the sense of property, but where mere consumption is concerned, we all of us feel a necessity, a craving, for enough and the continuance of enough. I have never met a man, I won't say who said, but I have never met a man who felt, that he wanted economic equality. I don't want it, and I don't think there is anybody in this room who wants it.

ONE IN THE AUDIENCE: Oh!

MR. BELLOC: No, economic equality, no. I don't believe there is anyone in this room who says: "I am comfortable; I have all I need; it will continue as long as I live, and my children shall have it after me—that is, five hundred a year—but how enviously I hate that man with a thousand a year!" That attitude of mind does not exist. That is not a human type. We do not feel thus about economic things, but we do feel to the marrow of our bones the desire for Sufficiency and Security. To say that we desire an absolute sufficiency is nonsense. You cannot define sufficiency. It is a certain minimum differing, I won't say with individuals, but certainly with traditions: and where the society is unhappily split, as English society is unhappily split, into various strata of differing traditions, you will find that within each stratum that feeling for the minimum is so strong that men brought up to a certain minimum, which is often far too much for any man really to want, will run the most terrible risks in order to obtain it for themselves and their children. As for security, every man born knows how strong the appetite for that is. Whether it be the thousand a year that a man is getting as Editor of a great newspaper of a Socialist tendency, or the hundred a year that a man is getting as a fairly skilled artisan, or the fourteen shillings a week which a man is getting as an agricultural labourer, once his standard is established, once his children are at least fed, clothed, housed—his domestic hearth founded on that basis—the security of it is essential to him and is perhaps the strongest craving he has. Very well. To establish a minimum security and a minimum sufficiency (you cannot get them absolute, and I do not pretend to define them) to meet in a substantial and sufficient way these two cravings is the work of any sane body of men in the economic sphere. When it fails on the economic side the body politic is sick. When it is absent, the body politic may be near its death and is certainly in a high fever. It is absent in England to-day. It is absent in North Germany, it is absent, especially in the original Puritan States of the United States, and there are patches of the cancer in France and in Italy, a few in Spain, and only one, I am glad to say, thank God, in Ireland. For this disease—which I may add, in passing, affects that part of the Lowlands between the Grampians and the high, deserted places of the Border—for this disease a remedy has been proposed to which a number of those now listening to me are attached, and to which Mr. MacDonald is attached. It is Collectivism. You say, and you are right in saying, that a phenomenon accompanying the insecurity and the insufficiency which the mass of men in industrial society feel to-day, and a phenomenon that is the proximate cause if not the ultimate cause of it, is the possession of the means of production by a minority. I have heard it denied, but I have never heard it denied by anybody who counted. I have heard it denied, but I have only heard it denied by the kind of people whose denial is a little help to any cause which they oppose—not a great help but a little help. And you propose—I say you; I am not addressing the audience at large; I never insult a large number of people, even when they are without weapons—but you that are Collectivists propose to settle this business by the putting of the means of production into the hands of the politicians, or, as you say, the community. The community is an abstraction; the politician is a reality, but no matter. I fully recognise this, that were you to do so the problem would be solved. Those of you who enjoy the full possession of your intelligence—I am not insulting you—will appreciate that there are other ideal, possible, hypothetical solutions. You may say that only yours is the practical one and the only one exactly consonant to the nature of man. You may say that millions of men naturally come together so easily, and so directly express their general view, that politicians will always obey them, even in detail. Perhaps I should agree, or perhaps not, but you cannot deny the mere theory that there are other solutions. One of those is the solution which has been attempted by the whole human race with the exception of those who have accepted the institution of slavery. The other is the solution which has been adopted by the whole human race where it has accepted the institution of slavery. The first solution is the seeing to it that a determining mass—I suppose in the ideal case every member—that at any rate the determining mass of society shall be possessed as individuals, or as corporations, regarded as free agents within the State, of the means of production. That was the ideal of the Middle Ages, and that is to-day the ideal, for instance, of China and of India. Another way of doing it—and it is that which I want to define—is the Servile State. You recognise, or if necessary you impose, a state of society in which the mass of your inhabitants—I won't say your citizens—are permanently dispossessed of the means of production. You differentiate the community into two classes, those who possess the means of production and those who do not. But you get security and sufficiency for all by organisation. You see to it, if you are humane, that the man who is not in possession of the means of production shall not be oppressed and that the punishments that will compel him to work are moderate and not excessive. You see to it that he lives the life which happens to suit your own particular ideal of the minimum of human comfort, but you do not put the means of production into his hands, directly or indirectly. He is a slave. Whether you use the word or whether you do not, that acceptation of one class permanently in possession of the means of production, and another side by side with it permanently dispossessed of the same, is what makes the Servile State, and that is what makes the slave class. And the other people, who own the means of production, you conversely, by the very act of creating a slave class, confirm in their possession of the means of production. You make them stronger in their citadel than before; you may prevent their being cruel; you may prevent everything which you do not like on the fringes of their action, but you do not take away their capital, and you do not take away their land. I hope I have defined the Servile State clearly. By my definition, if you should wake up to-morrow to find that all those millions of English men and women who possess no land or capital and who work at a weekly wage were confirmed in that wage for ever, and their children after them were looked after when in school, were looked after in old age. but never allowed to get capital or land, while, on the other hand the class that have it shall remain having it, you would wake up to find England not a Socialist State at all but a Servile State. Is that clear? Many people love that ideal. I do not say I dislike it. I have seen slaves in my life, and a greater man, if I may say so without egotism, Aristotle, was at the pains of remarking—I hope he did not mean it—something which the Catholic Church has denied with her dogmas—that certain men are born slaves. I do not say the Servile State is a bad thing, but at any rate it is not Collectivism. I was going to say it is not the S.D.F., but at any rate it is not Collectivism or Socialism. You are out—you who are Socialists are out—for a particular object, and I bear you this testimony, not as an opponent, but as a great sympathiser with all that is in your work parallel to the movement of democracy for the last hundred years; you not only fight for what is true, but you are capable of defending what you believe, and you desire to Collectivise, to Socialise to put into public hands—the hands of the politicians, that is—the means of production. If you do not do that, you fail, and the more you stereotype the state of society in which the community does not own the means of production, the more you have failed. The further you go from it, the further have you failed in Socialism. Very well. My next point, in the fourteen minutes that remain, is this. Out of the Servile State we came. There is no record of a Western European society which until the birth of that Personality which, by a private idiosyncrasy, I shall call Our Lord, was not upon a basis of servility, and I am not using the word servile—please remember this—in any bad sense. As Mr. MacDonald is a Scotchman, and therefore a clear thinker, I know he won't accuse me of that. It may be a very good thing to be a slave or to have slaves, or a slave class, or (by a prettier term) a servile class, just as it may be a nicer thing to have "labour colonies" than penal settlements for such of the proletariat as won't work for the capitalist. However. In what we—people like me—call, in our vulgar nomenclature, changed by the hypnosis of our religion, in what we call Pagan times. Western Europe reposed upon the servile basis. That was not only true of the civilised but also of the barbarian people. They could not think in other terms, just as Lloyd George cannot think in other terms. They had to think of employer and employed as being two different classes. They had to think of the freeman and the slave as distinct portions of the community. There fell upon that way of organising the economic business and that way of securing sufficiency and security—for those cravings were the human driving forces that produced slavery—a certain influence which I shall not be at length to define, for I am not here to talk history at any length, through history is the object lesson of all politics. Under this influence, that of the Catholic Church, the slave disappeared, and the disappearance of the servile class between, let us say, 600 to 700 and 1,300 and 1,400—in that slow process of seven or eight hundred years—is the big economic phenomenon of Western Europe. At the end of it the mass of Western European men, the determining mass of families, owned capital and land. It may be a bad thing for the man to own the house in which he lives, the soil which he tills, the instrument with which he works, either individually or co-operatively, in a guild, but anyhow free from the domination of his central government. Maybe it was bad to have men thus economically free—bad or good that society existed. And it broke down. It did not break down before a revolution in morals and in theology, but after a revolution in morals and in theology, and as a consequence of the revolution in morals and in theology. And after four hundred years of entertaining experiments, each of which has been more painful than the last, you are now arrived at a state of society which, in those countries which have abandoned tradition, you very well know cannot endure. I want to tell you people who think any province of Europe, even one so warped, can be transformed into a Collectivist society that as a matter of fact, when you deal with the material to your hand it turns all your efforts; and you transmute it (against your will) not into the Collectivist State, but into the Servile State. That is my point. Now what is the importance of that? If I were a Colonial, I should say that it had an importance from the point of view of Pragmatism, but being a civilised European I do not use terms of that sort. It is not of importance from the point of view of Pragmatism, because Pragmatism is bosh: it is a term used by people who do not use the grey matter of their brains, who do not "grip." The fact that you cannot and are not producing the Collectivist State has the importance which we all of us discover in any action of ours when we deal with the real universe. If, having learned too much or too little mathematics, but never having been to London, I say the straightest line from this hall here to St. Pancras, though it runs through a large number of houses is, in time, the shortest way to get there, experience will prove me to be wrong. If I pretend, as many young men do, that man is an absolute sort of being and that, let us say, ladies who have no votes have no power in the State, life will prove me to be wrong. If I pretend that good living, good eating, good drinking, heavy sleeping, happy holidays will make me happy at fifty, life will prove me to be wrong. That does not mean that logical deduction is a mistake, but that there is a very large number of first principles in the universe and that only God—if you will allow me to use the term—is capable of comprehending them all. That is the opposite of Pragmatism, because Pragmatism depends upon a pluralistic universe.

I now wish you to turn to this phenomenon, and I purposely put it at the end of this first section of the debate that I may gel matter for replying to from Mr. MacDonald. You have laboriously built up, in books, in journalism, and in some, at least, of the Parliaments—they're none of them worth much—of Western Europe a Socialist propaganda. And at what have you arrived by it? You have municipal enterprise. You have it only by borrowing from the capitalist. You have never confiscated; you have never dared to confiscate; you have never tried to confiscate. You borrow from the capitalist, and you offer the capitalist interest upon his capital, whether the enterprise pays or whether it does not. You point to those enterprises, with their sinking funds of course, but you have in Western Europe as a whole, this. When you began all this wonderful work, the capitalist had not got his grip to any large extent upon the municipalities and corporate life of the towns of Western Europe. To-day you are earning—according to statistics; you can play with them, but roughly it is this—you are earning 1.8 per cent, and you are paying 3.2 per cent. You do not only borrow tramcars, copper wires and granite setts for tramways which pay, you also borrow very largely for experiments that do not pay, for wash-houses that hardly pay, for libraries that are not intended to pay; you borrow bricks, mortar, tiles, glass, at interest, although these things do not breed. There has been no advance towards that prime action, that virile thing, without which Socialism is worthless—confiscation. And not only have you not begun it, but you are going further and further away from it. Last night, in the House of Commons, there was brought in a Bill which is roughly to this effect, and I believe it is accepted by what is called "all parties" (which always means a tiny minority of the English people), you are going by this Bill to put for the purposes of insurance against the accidents of modern capitalism—in other words, for establishing security to the capitalist on his side and the proletarian on his—£9,200,000 of taxation per year on the shoulders of the working classes. You are going to put a somewhat smaller taxation upon the shoulders of the employing classes: and what is called the State, that is, every man who drinks a glass of beer or cup of tea, or smokes a pipe of tobacco, is going to provide something more. There are individuals who would resist that kind of thing, but you Socialists will accept it, and you will be by that step further from the ideal of Collectivism. You cannot but be further from it. It is not my ideal. I am not here to-night defending it or opposing it. You know very well that personally I am opposed to it, but at any rate my argument stands, that if your ideal were consonant to the nature of man, and if this putting of the means of production into the hands of the politicians were a normal, a safe, solution of the problem, as contrasted with—though I am not introducing that to-night; that is a side issue, but it is perhaps the main issue of all—as contrasted with the proper distribution of the means of production in ownership, co-operative and private, throughout the people; then that Collectivist ideal fails in this, that when you begin to legislate and try to apply it to men, your instruments slip off their material. The tool slips off the metal. Your theory is not chosen with a knowledge of the stuff with which it has to deal, and human nature, in all its little ways and instincts, pushes you off into something other and worse than you intended. Catch my argument well before I sit down. I have still exactly a minute. My argument is this. All your reforms which touch the proletariat in industrial society tend, not to a Collectivist State at all, but to a Servile State; that is, to a State in which the mass not to-day possessed, and increasingly for the last four hundred years dispossessed, in industrial Europe, of the means of production shall be confirmed in sufficiency and security, in having enough and in being sure of having enough; but shall not advance at all towards the possession, collectively or individually, of the means of production. That is my point. And I add as corollary to that plain fact which all can see before them that this fact is a proof that your theory which demands the Collectivising or Socialising of the means of production is as a workable and human thing untrue. It does not work with the stuff of humanity. Very well. That is my thesis, and I want Mr. MacDonald in his reply, only for my sake and the sake of the audience, to avoid three things, I do not want him to say it is an aid to Collectivism to create a servile class, because it is not. When you make a very large number of people, millions of people, comfortable you are not making people who will rebel against capitalists. Secondly, I hope he won't say—because it will give me a lot of trouble for nothing—that these movements towards the Servile State are not there, because they are. If he says in his reply that they are not, then in my reply I shall bring a certain number of things which I think will startle him, not only from this country but from Germany and from France. Thirdly, I do not want him to say that the Servile State actually is the Collectivist State, because it isn't.

MR. RAMSAY MACDONALD: Mr. Chairman and friends, it is always a great pleasure to meet my friend Belloc, whether it is at dinner or in debate. He has been genial, he has been facetious, he has been original, he has been obscure, but never-the less I think he has committed a sufficient amount of indiscretions and promulgated a sufficient number of errors to give me an opportunity of asking you to listen to me for half-an-hour. He had, as you will have noticed, a glimmering idea—whether it was rational or conscientious I do not quite know—before he sat down as to what lines my reply was to go upon, and like an old and well-trained soldier he took the precaution to tell me that if I replied as I ought to reply he would consider it was no reply at all. Well, Belloc and I are old friends, and I will draw upon that friendship to tell him that I am going to reply in my own way. We are told that we do not mean to land you in the Servile State. We say the opposite. We believe the opposite, but as a matter of fact, says Mr. Belloc, you are going into the Servile State. He just reminds me of a man looking over George Bernard Shaw's shoulder when he is writing one of his immortal plays, and without having read the play from the beginning, and without having seen the magnificent ending of the play, he says "Bless me, what is the man scrawling about? There is no play there. I see a few irregular things" and those of us who have had correspondence with Shaw know the very irregular and undecipherable things that look like letters—"I see a few irregular things, but it is no play at all." Of course, the reply that Shaw would immediately make to this man, and the reply that I make to Belloc, is that you never can judge what is happening if you take a process of evolution at any given moment and say "I am just going to study it there." You should begin away back. You evolve towards an end. But, says Mr. Belloc, if my opponent urges that argument I am going to say that is not argument, and I am going to insist upon my opponent drawing a little line here and there, and confining the whole of his argument and attention within this narrow and incomplete field. I submit to Mr. Belloc that if he seriously means to stand by that argument he gives a very good reason why he has been using the expression Servile State to-night so frequently, with, I submit, so little meaning. Now what does he say? He began quite truly by stating that nobody ever suggested that Socialism meant economic equality. That is perfectly true. Then he made another true statement. He says what we want is sufficiency, which he says is one thing to one man and another thing to another man. That is perfectly true, because sufficiency is not economic at all, but psychological. But psychological sufficiency must always have an economic basis or an economic medium for expressing itself. Then, after having laid down that truth, he departed upon a very characteristic Bellockian error, by saying that this sufficiency was equivalent to a demand that each, one and all, severally and separately, should own his own means of production.

MR. BELLOC: No.

MR. MACDONALD: But that is the only argument. That is one of the sticks I have handed over to you to beat my back with when your twenty minutes come. We will see about that. That is the only meaning that I can attach to it, but if Mr. Belloc rejects that interpretation then I will begin with his own argument. You want a sufficiency. Precisely; I agree; that is common ground. How are you going to get it? You cannot possibly get it by each of you owning your own acre of land, your own house, you own bit of Armstrong, Whitworth & Company's machinery, your own Member of Parliament, your own Editor, your own newspaper, and your own constituency. You cannot do it. You might have done it in those delightful primitive days in which my friend Belloc's mind has taken up what, I am sorry to say, seems to be a sort of permanent abode and habitation, but a man of modern mind, modern tendencies, and modern rationality cannot possibly take up that position. What happened in those deplorable days when there was a revolution in mind and in morals—I think that is Belloc's expression; it not, he will correct me in those twenty minutes—what happened in those days when the revolution in mind and in morals started? You emerged not merely from one moral point of view to another, and from one religious form of organisation and belief to another, you also emerged from one economic organisation, one form of economic and industrial organisation, to another, and the one that you went into was one which was characterised by a great mass of capital being used as an economic unity by a great mass of men co-ordinated. . . .

MR. BELLOC: No.

MR. MACDONALD: Yes, co-ordinated into a social unit, and whilst your production was co-operative and communal, your distribution was individualistic on the old-fashioned mediæval lines. What happened was this.

You did not have a complete revolution in mind and in morals and in society. You had a piecemeal revolution. You solved the problem of production in a modern way, but you failed to apply your modern minds and circumstances to the problem of distribution. What does the Socialist say? The Socialist says there is no use talking about individualism and production again. When you talk of the common ownership of the means of production, distribution, and exchange, that does not mean that you are dividing it all up into so many parcels and then handing it out over a post.-office counter as you get your old age pensions now. Nothing of the kind. It means that you keep it co-ordinated, organised, working co-operatively, and that that thing which Mr. Belloc thinks is an abstraction when it does not mean merely a politician, the community, should own that, control it, and see that it is used for the benefit of the separate individual who is using it as a co-operating factor. That is the Socialist State. And why use in connection with that State the expression Politician? Is it to enlighten you or to mislead you? Is it an accurate description or a prejudiced description? I venture to say that it is used to mislead you, and that it is a prejudiced description. Because why a politician? I am certain that my friend Belloc knows as well as I do that the Socialist State is not going to be only a political State; that is the mistake that ignorant people like Mr. Mallock make, not learned people like Mr. Belloc make. The Socialist State is a State which is not merely political, as the modern State mainly is. It is rapidly becoming something else. It is a State which I at any rate think must always be political but which must also be industrial, and you are going to have the two organisations, the two absolutely different types of organisation, the Industrial State and the Political State, not existing side by side, because that is a false analogy, but interfused one into another, the one impregnating the other, so to speak, the two blended together to make a genuine Democratic State—democratic on its political side, democratic on its industrial side—owning those forms of capital in the use and abuse of which the whole community is more interested than any private individual, and then establishing a system of distribution which will enable the co-operating producer to consume as a self-regarding and self-contained moral and rational individual. Now you cannot bring that about, and you cannot have a clear conception of how it is going to be brought about, unless your mind refuses to go upon political lines and goes upon industrial lines. Instead of the politician which Mr. Belloc has asked you to think about and to concentrate your attention upon, think of the manager of a successful co-operative business. The blending of Parliament and the Co-operative Union of Manchester must take place.

MR. BELLOC: Heaven help us !

MR. MACDONALD: I knew that that expression was comming. He says "Heaven help us." Well, I think we have not quite come to that yet. I think we can help ourselves, quite apart from Heaven, and my reason for saying that is this, that an intelligent man like Belloc knows all the difficulties in the way. That is why. If we were going blindly on, thinking that our present political condition was the best we could devise, going blindly on thinking the Co-operative Union was the best that could be devised, then Belloc's pessimistic interjection would be perfectly justifiable. But as we see clearly how we are going to amend both, and as there is a vast amount of experience accumulating which will enable us to amend both, and as we are beginning as a matter of actual fact, experiments to amend both, then we have not come yet to the pessimistic exclamation of "Heaven help us." We are helping ourselves, and we are evolving that state of society under which the industrial idea of co-operation and the political idea of representative government can be blended and used for both political and industrial purposes. That is not the Servile State. The Servile State is a State which depends, not upon production at all, but upon consumption. Servility does not depend upon a system under which a man produces, unless his personal liberty happens to be sacrificed to the production, and his personal liberty even then must always be limited by his social personality and not by his more eccentric and individualistic personality. Keeping these things in mind, we then have got to reply to the Servile State idea that under Socialism, whilst the means of production may be held in common, the means of consumption will be held individually, and the man who defines that State as the Servile State is only abusing the English language. That is my State. The final point that I have got here, when I was asked to reply to certain things so that the coming twenty minutes might be filled up, is this. Says Mr. Belloc, we have never confiscated anything yet, and therefore we are no good. Well, we have confiscated a good many things. I will tell you what we have confiscated. We have confiscated a shilling in the £ of Belloc's income. And if he's fortunate enough to have any of his income invested in the Funds, we have confiscated a little bit more. If he is fortunate enough, from an economic point of view, to own building land round about London, we have confiscated more still. If he is fortunate enough to have an income of fifteen thousand a year we have confiscated still more. I congratulate my friend that from his economic resources he can shake that mournful head of his so as to indicate that he has been touched on all these points. But, he says, when you do all your work, all your public work, your municipal trams, and so on, you only do it on borrowed capital. Precisely. How long does borrowed capital exist? It does not exist more than twenty years at the very outside. His argument is not quite sound, but I am not going to go into details. I am going to assume it, which after all is the best way to deal with it. I am going to assume that his argument is sound. Even if we borrow for the purpose of building our schools with bricks and mortar, what happens? The ground is ours when the loans are paid off; the bricks and mortar are ours when the loans are paid off; and if we go on sufficiently long—mark you, I am not using this as my argument, but only showing that his argument is unsound—if we go on sufficiently long the process of borrowing is a terminable process, and the weight of the borrowed money is a constantly diminishing weight, until even on that line, if we adopt it, an intelligent statesman will at last bring you to Socialism and clear the borrowing out altogether. Really, from the point of view of the debate, I am prepared to leave it there. I believe I still have a quarter of an hour, but so far as the real points were concerned, and so far as the attack upon Socialism was concerned, I think I have made my reply. I want to know, however, what Belloc exactly has got in his mind. He talks about the Servile State. What does he mean by the Servile State? He said he defined it, but he did not. He says the Servile State is a State under which the means of production are not held by the people, but that is not the Servile State. I might claim that that is the Collectivist State. Will he tell me what is the difference between that Collectivist State and the Servile State?

MR. BELLOC: Oh yes.

MR. MACDONALD: Then he tells us that he goes back to the Middle Ages, to the days of the Guilds and so on. Will he tell us how it is possible under modern conditions, with factories and factory production and large capitalism, to go back to the conditions under which the Guilds flourished? Will he tell me exactly what idea of production he has got, what idea of capitalism he has got, and what idea of Socialist organisation he has got? Will he tell me how he is going to build that up, how he is going to move into that from the present state of society in which he finds himself? If he is going to upset the factory system, will he tell me how he is going to do it? If he is going to break up co-ordinated and unified capital, will he tell me how? If he is going to divide up his units so that he adopts the Guild idea, will he tell me how much of the Guild idea he will adopt, and what sort of a social fabric he is going to create at the end? As a matter of fact, I contend first of all that Belloc's line of argument is unscientific, because he does not allow for the evolutionary process, the working out of the Socialist idea through time. The words he uses are mere labels and do not signify reality at all, like the expression Collectivism, as he uses it, on the one hand,

and the expression Servile and Servility, as he uses it, on the other—meaningless. On the other hand he has not told us where he himself stands and what cure he proposes to offer for the various social evils with which we are faced. I maintain that the Socialist idea of Collectivism, of taking what we call capital—and I use the word because I do not want to confuse and explain issues—I maintain that the Socialist idea that you must have co-operative production by massed capital, by massed labour, and then alongside of that that you must create some system of distribution, which Socialism can do and tells you how you can do, is the only rational, the only possible, and the only hopeful way of solving the social difficulties with which we are now faced.

MR. BELLOC: Every institution is fitted to the nation in which it arises.

ONE IN THE GALLERY: Speak up.

MR. BELLOC: I shall begin quite differently now. I don't want to be like a lawyer, but if you will allow me I cannot help being precise. It is my nature. I affirmed the following proposition: "That the unreality of the Collectivist ideal is apparent from the fact that contemporary Collectivist effort is leading, not to Collectivism, but to the Servile State." I then defined this abstraction, the Servile State, in order that my words might have some meaning. Since I am told that my definition was nebulous I will repeat it. The Servile State is that in which a portion of the community is permanently dispossessed of the means of production and is compelled to labour and to produce for the advantage, not only of themselves, but also of those privileged beings who retain the means of production. And when I say compelled I do not mean more or less elbowed into such labour, but compelled to it by law. For instance, by Lloyd George's law a man may pay fourpence a week out of that £9,200,000, week after week and year after year, out of his eighteen shillings a week at the docks, but there may come a day when he does not accept employment under the terms offered by the Labour Exchanges, in which case he sacrifices the sum. I think I have defined myself clearly. That is the Servile State. I did not say it was a bad thing. All of us have ancestors who owned slaves, and all of us have ancestors who were slaves. There is no man in this room who, two thousand years ago, had not an ancestor who owned slaves, or an ancestress, and there is not a man in this room who had not one who was a slave or a slaveress, a she-slave. I do not say that the Servile State is a bad thing. The society in which Greek tragedy arose was a far better society than that of modern England, and if you say "I like a slave state; I am asking for a slave state," I should say "I thoroughly understand you; go ahead. I differ, because I am one of the old guard; I believe in God, and so forth; but go ahead and make your slave state and say that everybody shall have bread and butter and food, and do not bother too much whether the capitalist class is secure in its predominance so long as the servile class is secure in its mere sufficiency." But Mr. MacDonald did not meet that point. He said I was obscure. I wish I was. I will re-define myself as clearly as possible. I will begin again. The Servile State is one in which a portion of the inhabitants of the State, dispossessed of the means of production, are secure in sufficiency, without the dispossession of the capitalist or means-of-production-owning class. Is that clear? I ask Mr. MacDonald in the clearest way this. You have been at it for seventy years. Our Lord—if you will pardon me the term; I almost said Our Blessed Lord—died about the year 33 or the year 37. The Neronian persecution took place, I think, about a generation later, and about a hundred years later the thing we now call the Catholic Church was fully grounded. Where is your Socialism? You have had about seventy years to Collectivise property. Are you getting nearer or farther? When I was a boy of nineteen and did not know the world, I went through the gas strike and the great dock strike of 1889, with John Burns, by the way, incredible as it may seem. I did not meet him much; I won't pretend to be a follower of a much more important man than myself; but I met him once or twice. Though my motives are the same to-day as they were then, I cannot but look back upon that time and say to myself that we are farther from actual confiscation than we were then. We are putting water in our wine, and we are getting contented, and part of our content is the putting of £9,200,000 of direct taxation upon the proletariat of England. What have you transferred; what have you begun to transfer? What step have you taken, MacDonald—you and yours—in the direction of transferring the means of production from those who own into the hands of those who do not own, individually or collectively?

MR. MACDONALD: Income tax.

MR. BELLOC: No. Income tax does not fall upon capital; that is the point. I own capital, and I own land. You have not touched my capital and my land. He said he had confiscated so much out of a shilling of my income. I despair when on an economic matter requiring a clear definition and clear thought—a scientific matter—a leader of economic thought comes forward and calls that the confiscation of the means of production. You have not advanced one step towards getting the land or towards getting the capital. You have in some cases taken capital by mistake, as in the unfortunate licensing clauses of Lloyd George's remarkable Budget. But you have not applied it to buying the means of production. You spend it on salaries to the new people of the Bureaucracy that you are creating. If you were to earmark—recommend this to him, that he will earmark the death duties of 1912, that he will move that they be earmarked for the purchase of the railways that run south of London. If he will do that I shall approve, because railways I—in common with Justinian, who did not know about railways but who knew about roads—agree in regarding as things normally national. Then he will at least have transferred the means of production—at any rate, capital—from the hands of private people and put certain means of production by something very like confiscation in the hands of the State. Now there has not been a trace of such a policy in any country in Europe to the present day. Mr. MacDonald says borrowed capital will be repaid shortly by the terms of its loan. He says we are paying back. It is true of every individual loan that it carries a sinking fund, but that shows nothing: the point is whether the total indebtedness of Communities to Capital is rising or no.

Members of this audience, some few of you may have passed through that experience that has coloured the whole of my life, in which you had to borrow, and I will ask you: Is it your own experience that the creditor is especially kind at the point where his investment begins to be difficult? Give him an inch—does he not take an ell? When a man borrows and puts a sinking fund on to his borrowing, if he is a capable man, still with power, he may ultimately pay back his private debt. Many have done so. What are your Collectivities under the so-called Socialist pressure of the Socialist politicians doing? Why, the debt is increasing and increasing. It has increased to such a point that now the investor is beginning to say: "We won't lend you any more." Where is your sinking fund then? You borrow money for pageants, you borrow money for what Ruskin called "fireworks," you borrow money for mistakes in tramlines—even those poor devils of tramlines that have to carry the whole burden of the argument, even they sometimes do not pay. You are receiving 1.8 per cent, at the best; you are paying 3.2 per cent, at the lowest. I am talking of what is, not of what might be. If there were an infinite power of borrowing always with a good investment, you would, of course, at last pay off, but do you think the capitalist class is going to allow you to do that? You are going to take their wealth without fighting, without initiative? I used the phrase "Heaven help us." I won't say it would need something more than Heaven, but it would need a great effort on the part of Heaven. You won't get hold of the means of production save on the barricades. But you have not begun to do it even in your legislation. I shall believe this argument of repayment when I see the debt diminishing, but I do not. It is increasing, and that debt, vaguely called Municipal Debt, is owed to somebody. To whom? To the capitalist, whom, by the way, one may never attack by name.

ONE IN THE AUDIENCE: What about the National Debt?

MR. BELLOC: That is exactly in the same category. When it is spent on railways, with a sinking fund, it is wisely spent; when it is spent on fireworks it is unwisely spent, but in every case it is owed to the capitalist class and is a millstone round the neck of the producer. Now I have exhausted twelve or thirteen minutes, and I want Mr. MacDonald in his second reply to get to that precise point. If we are getting towards Collectivism, well and good. Let him give me instances of it. But if he says we are not getting towards the Servile State, I will give him a few instances which will make him think. Take Western Europe as a whole. The other day the Rothschilds in France quarrelled with their workmen. The Socialist Press called the Rothschilds in this connection the "Compagnie du Nord." They quarrelled with their workmen over twopence a week. I should not say this if they could send me to prison for saying it—I am taking care not to tell you the whole truth. They quarrelled with their workmen over twopence a week. The workmen came out on strike, and they thought—poor innocents!—that their right as free men to work or not to work was an unbreakable weapon. "We," they said, "hold the means of communication, at least between one Province of France and the Capital.. We will come out, and we must win." Did they? A politician and a leader of the proletariat and a strong Socialist of the name of Briand ordered them under pain of death to go back and work. He did not order the Rothschilds under pain of death to give up that twopence. I am not a Socialist, but if I had been at that conference and I had been Briand, I do not think Rothschild would have enjoyed his dinner again. You see what I mean? Armed with a human motive, nerved with a human purpose, you can do something; with these German-Jewish abstractions you can do nothing at all. I ask again: What have you Socialists done—how far have you proceeded? I want Mr. MacDonald to answer that. Have we, as a fact, come any nearer to his ideal; have we not come nearer to the Servile State? In the four minutes remaining, let me say—and I shall only occupy two of them—there is another argument, and I am astonished that Mr. MacDonald has not used it. I paid him the compliment of saying he was Scotch, and upon my soul when I hear him talking I think he must be from Huntingdonshire, which was, as this intelligent and well-educated audience knows, for a long time a Scotch fief. There is an argument, and I wonder he did not use it. He might have said "Yes, we are working for the Servile State: but "when we have produced the Servile State then you will see we shall have the Collectivist State as the next stage." I ask you as a mere matter of human psychology how the one can lead to the other, and I ask him to take that point. You may have created a state of society in which, from one generation to another, the minority are used to their confirmation and security in the means of production, with all its advantages, and a large majority are used to and secure in what they need for their own little lives, but not to ownership and not to the responsibility that comes with ownership. "When you have produced that State, have you produced a national psychology which will lead to revolt and the taking away of the means of production from the rich? Of course not. You have produced a nation comfortable and used to servile conditions. This may be very good. I am not blaming it. But you have gone right out of the path that leads to collectivism. I happen to believe that if property were well distributed, you would automatically, as is proved to be the case ever since history began, have arising in the organism of human society co-operative institutions each safeguarding itself against too great competition. But I am not debating that to-night. I am telling you that the drift of actual, so-called Socialist legislation is not towards Socialism at all, but towards this established, confirmed, and secure division—between owners and non-owners, which I predicate as the great danger of modern industrial society.

MR MACDONALD: I am very sorry that I have to go back to the Servile State again. The proposition which Mr. Belloc is affirming to-night is, as he quoted, "That the unreality of the Collectivist ideal is apparent from the fact that contemporary Collectivist effort is leading, not to Collectivism, but to the Servile State."I asked him to define what he meant by the Servile State. He says it is a State in which a small section of the community own the means of production ....

MR. BELLOC: Are confirmed in the ownership of the means of production.

MR. MACDONALD: But if they are confirmed in the ownership, do not they own it? ... in which a small section of the community own the means of production, and if Belloc likes I will add, and are confirmed in their ownership. That is precisely the state of things to-day.

MR. BELLOC: It is really putting my words wrong. I added: "And those who do not own are confirmed insufficiency and security under the owners."

MR. MACDONALD: But the Servile State does not require that the slaves should be confirmed in sufficiency. What Belloc means to do is to create something which is very special to his own ideas and then call that something the Servile State; but never mind. Let us have it. That is precisely what is happening at the present moment, and it is against that that the whole of the Collectivist movement is being aimed. What is happening? How can Mr. Belloc assume that Collectivism and that definition of the Servile State of his are one and the same thing, when as a matter of fact the whole trend of modern Collectivism is to put an end to the ownership of the means of production by a small section of the community? Mr. Belloc says: "Show me what you are doing for Collectivism." Very well; the question is perfectly simply answered, but first of all let me ask Belloc whether he precisely understands what kind of contribution Socialism requires at the present moment. He might have come to me if we had both been living in 1831—he an old Tory and myself, say, a Radical—and he might have come and challenged me with all his eloquence and with all his falsity of logic, in 1831, and said: "I challenge you to show me one single step you have taken towards the extension of the franchise in this country. You have been working for it since 1780; this is 1831; that is about 60 years—(A voice : "Forty years"*)

—"and now," he would say, "after all this agitation, after all this strife, you are just as far away from it as ever you were before." Is there a single piece of finished work about which precisely the same thing cannot be said? He turns and he says he was surprised I did not reply that through the Servile State we are coming to Collectivism. I did not reply that because I deny the reality of his definition of the Servile State. I did as a matter of fact reply on precisely the lines he said he expected a reply, but which he thought he did not get, when I instanced the writing of the play of the friend in front of me to my left-hand side (Mr. G. Bernard Shaw). Now before you get Collectivism you have got to get a Collectivist intention and will in the people outside. Does Belloc mean to say that at the present moment there is not more Collectivist intention, enormously more, in this country than there was when he took part in the great dock strike behind Burns? Why, nowadays the great difficulty that we have all got to experience is that you cannot get anybody to stand upon theory against Collectivist and Socialist ideas. Everything that "is done now, whether by reactionary people or by so-called progressive people, is being done upon the assumption that the community as a whole has got power, has got wealth, has got responsibility, and ought to take co-operative action. Confiscation, says Belloc, is further away now than it was when he was a boy of nineteen. I am glad of it, because if Mr. Belloc and the handful of people who associate with him and share his opinions—I differentiate between the handful of people who share his opinions and the vast number of people who delight

---

* Mr. Belloc would not have been good at mathematics.—J.R.M.

in reading about his opinions, of which I am one â€" if Belloc imagines that he is going to measure the rapidity of the coming of Socialism or Collectivism by the amount of confiscation that is being done, then of course he and I disagree absolutely and fundamentally. We are not going to get to Socialism by confiscation, as he calls it, unless he means by confiscation what I mean by income tax. What did the State do to entitle it to claim from Mr. Belloc the money that he thought was his own? Absolutely nothing—from the point of view of the person who believes in confiscation, mark you. The State stepped in and said: "Mr. Belloc. you pay your money, your property, your income into your bank every year to a certain amount. I will confiscate one- fourth or one-fifth of it, as the case may be, and I take it to myself." What is the use of Mr. Belloc using the word confiscation if he is not going to apply it when it actually takes place? That is not all. The whole of our municipal experiments are going on and have been created—our parks, our municipal housing schemes, our municipal tramway schemes; aye, even this scheme of insurance, imperfect as it is and as we know it is, a scheme of insurance for which a Liberal Government is responsible, and not a Collectivist Government; nevertheless, ten years ago that scheme, with all its faults and all its shortcomings, would have been far too Collectivist for even a Liberal Government to have brought into operation. In fact, Belloc's argument narrows itself down to this. He says: "To-day you have not got Socialism." Well, nobody has ever said we had. And when you work it down, analyse the argument to its contents, and give it an accurate meaning, that is all it comes to, that after so many years of agitation, and organisation, and legislation, we have not yet got Socialism. But why? Because you are in a minority. Mr. Belloc does not only want confiscation. That is a pretty tall order, and it is a very queer order. He says he is not a Socialist; his speech shows that, and his criticism of Socialism shows it. He will have a chance of becoming a Socialist when he ceases to imagine that Socialism is going to come by confiscation. But he does not only want confiscation; he also wants a minority to rule the majority, because only under that political condition would it be possible for the Collectivist minority to-day to show you any pure scheme or experiment in Collectivism. What is happening and what is bound to happen? It is no use people living in a social vacuum. What you have to do is this. You have to remember where your Socialism started, under what conditions it started, and you have to remember the transforming process, both in its kind and in its nature, which has to take place before your Socialist movement can really triumph over the conditions that it wants to take the place of. You start from capitalism, the ordinary capitalism, the content of which we all know perfectly well. We start as a critical organisation, very crude at first, using absolute expressions, which we by-and- by apply under capitalism, not under Socialism, which we by-and-by apply in the actual world, not in the ideal world which we have constructed in our own minds; and in the application of those ideas of ours we are limited, not by ourselves, but by you. We are limited, not by Socialist opinion, but by opinion outside, by Mr. Belloc, for instance, who is not a Socialist at all. We have got to take into account all the possibilities and only the possibilities which are at our disposal for practical legislative purposes, and if when the experiments that we can conduct are being made a critic should rise up and say they are not perfect, well, of course they are not perfect; they are just as much as society will stand, and their imperfections of to-day will be smoothed out by amendments and changes to-morrow, and there is not a single Socialist with any common sense who believes in any other method except that.

MR. BELLOC: What about the railways!"

MR. MACDONALD: Well, take the railways. Thirty years ago the railways were the subject of an enormously entrenched organisation of private interests. What has happened? We have just had a committee reporting, consisting not of Socialists, not even of Labour men—there was only one Labour man on the committee—but consisting of railway magnates, capitalists, business men, and that committee has issued a report which was published three days ago and which foreshadowed in every page railway nationalisation. Take canals. We have had a canal commission sitting since 1906, with one Socialist upon it: Chairman, Lord Shuttleworth; Lord Farrer a Member, Sir John Brunner a member, and men of that type. What has happened? Your committee has reported that you ought to have an efficient canal service, that you have not got an efficient canal service, and that if you are going to get an efficient canal service, you have got to nationalise the whole service and find the money for it. These things have got to be done. You have got to change public opinion before you can re-write history and change the social organisation of the country, and I claim that that is being done. Mr. Belloc knows very well—I think at any rate he does, sitting as a Member of Parliament—that time after time when we discussed industrial and socialist things the trouble always was that there was a certain section in the House of Commons calling themselves social reformers who always tried their best to say as much as we said. Why? Because they were beginning to be conscious of the fact that the whole mental outlook of our people is changing. As a matter of fact, we are going through precisely the same revolution, or a revolution of the same kind, as that to which Belloc referred in his opening speech as the revolution of the Middle Ages. From being individualists We are becoming Socialists; socialistic first of all, and then Socialists. We are going to ensure against unemployment first of all. That is the first step.

Mr. Belloc interjected a remark.

MR. MACDONALD: Yes, it may be expensive work, but we are not living in heaven.

MR. BELLOC: No, I said at the expense of the workers.

MR. MACDONALD: It may he, but even then that is only a superficial view to take of it. If I am going to create, even at the expense of the workers, a system of social responsibility which will evolve by a law of its own being into a real system of social responsibility, financed from social sources, and not used as a burden upon the workers, then I am going to take and make the beginning that public opinion to-day will allow me, and when we get into Committee on this Bill we are going to change some of the Bill. I venture to say that if this debate were to take place six months from now instead of to-night....

MR. BELLOC: I will take it on.

MR. MACDONALD: And I will be delighted to accept. I was saying that if this debate had taken place six months from now instead of to-night you would have found that as a result of the Labour Party criticism, the Collectivist criticism, both from the Labour Party and outside the Labour Party, this scheme that we would then be considering would be far better moulded in a Collectivist likeness than it is at present. Of course, Mr. Belloc can criticise what is known as Socialistic Liberalism or Social Reform Liberalism. So can 1. So we all do, and so do the Socialists all round. But the difference between him and myself is this, that he will accept nothing as Socialism except the finished product, whereas I say, that that is not the problem at all. The problem is: Are you going first of all in the direction of changing public opinion, and secondly, of applying that changed public opinion to your social work? Are you going out in a Socialist direction?' I maintain that in thirty years the change has been enormous. No man can close his eyes to the fact that it exists, and consequently so far as Collectivism is concerned my contention is that first of all it is alien even to Belloc's own definition of the Servile State, that as a matter of fact his Servile State is not being created, but that the real fact is that Collectivism is being steadily applied to transform capitalism and in that transforming stage, that sort of transition stage, it is bound to be badly applied, it is bound to be imperfect, it is bound in some respects to be disappointing, but there beyond the change Collectivism is coming stronger and stronger and stronger and will ultimately emerge triumphant.

MR. BELLOC: The last five minutes of this type of debate, which, like silk, is imported from France, hardly ever has to do with arguments in this country, but with re-stating one's opinions. The gist of Mr. MacDonald's reply, I think I may say, was this. We have not got a Socialist State, but all these various moves towards giving the proletariat security and not capital, and the employers security and not confiscation, are moves towards the Socialist State. That is evolution. I submit, I only submit, that in my philosophy, and only in my philosophy and that of the handful of men who agree with me, there is a difference between south and north, between dark and light, between plus and minus; and if such differences exist, then the whole point of the Servile State is that it is walking away from the Collectivist State. You are producing, by things like the Insurance Bill, a state of society in which England wants to help the poor, in which people feel kind towards the poor, and in which people are willing to put £9,200,000 burden of direct taxation on the shoulders of the poor, but you are emphatically not approaching towards the confiscation of the means of production. Mr. MacDonald says he does not want to confiscate the means of production. Tell it to your children, and to your children's children. He is going to get the means of production out of the hands of the rich without confiscation, by Parliamentary means, by good-fellowship and practical understanding of men and of human affairs. Twice to-night I have used the phrase: "Heaven help us." I add: Heaven help the human intellect if such confused thought can determine affairs. It is true that you can so affect the gradual economic processes of society—that is quite true—as to canalise them in this or that direction. It is true that a great statesman possessed of great powers, perhaps almost of despotic powers, can save society by that method. It is true, and I grant that fully, that you can produce the Collectivist State in that fashion. You could, by perpetually taxing income up to the breaking point, and always transferring the proceeds to the purchase of the means of production, begin to produce the Socialist State. But my whole point is that there is not a sign of its coming into being. So-called "Socialistic" legislation takes nineteen to twenty millions pounds in death duties from the rich in a year, and then, instead of transforming it into nationally-owned land or capital, pays it away in salaries to the hungry people who hang upon the party system and upon their subordinates: the politicians pay it to bureaucrats. Bureaucrats are very useful, but they are not the means of production. Why does not Mr. MacDonald move (what I am perfectly prepared to move) whenever in the House of Commons you can move anything, and he is a leader of a party and can do it—the earmarking of the death duties for the purpose of purchasing the railways? Why not?

ONE IN THE AUDIENCE: It would cost eleven millions.

MR. BELLOC: Why do they call it Collectivism or the national ownership of the means of production to take this money and spend it on salaries? Obviously it is not. Now there is another point which is well worth emphasising. Mr. MacDonald appeals to what is of real value in this debate, namely, experience in the House of Commons. I had five years of it. I left it voluntarily, and if I return it will be more voluntarily still. He tells me that I had experience, sitting there as a Radical, that the trouble was to prevent reactionary people from stopping this flood of modern Socialist feeling. It was nothing of the sort.

MR. MACDONALD: I did not say that. I said expressing themselves, that when reactionary people wanted to fight us they expressed themselves in the language we used.

MR. BELLOC: I am to blame, and Mr. MacDonald is quite right. The trouble was, as one may say familiarly, to pin them down. They always used our terminology, they admitted the existence of land, and they were good enough to say that machinery was to be discovered in this world. Do you know what it is impossible to get through the House of Commons? I will tell you, and with that I shall sit down. You may think it has nothing to do with this debate, but I have only two minutes, and not even that by rights, in which to tell you the following anecdote. If you think it does not apply to the debate, then you are of a different lineage and atavism from myself. A law was proposed by Mr. Herbert Gladstone, now Lord Gladstone—that great name is now dignified with a peerage—and that law is now being administered by that son of the people Mr. Winston Churchill, and that other independent democrat Mr. Masterman, and what does that law say? That law says that any man guilty three times of petty "larceny, stealing a pocket handkerchief, poaching, getting a few eggs out of a ne.st, after the full and maximum sentence which the law allows him, may be kept in prison for five years apart from the company of all human beings and apart from human speech, and womenfolk—in Hell—to teach him not to steal pocket handkerchiefs and birds' nests. The first man who was sent to do these extra five years was a man who stole an india-rubber mat. The mat was worth three-and-six. You talk about the weakening of the old defence of property; you talk of the advance of Socialist ideas which denies the right to such monopolies. But which of you opposed that law? I fought it in the House of Commons—God remember it for me at the last day—tooth and nail. I got an indefinite sentence down to five years—but when it came to dividing against that infamous thing, which stinks in the nostrils of what is left of Christendom in Europe—that infamous thing—I could get no one in the House of Commons to "tell" with me. That is the House of Commons.

MR. MACDONALD: I want to begin where Belloc ended, The picture he has given of the House of Commons is absolutely inaccurate and altogether a caricature.

MR. BELLOC: Who "told" with me on that question?

MR. MACDONALD: The question that he has raised finally is one which cannot be dealt with in live minutes, but the theory of detention which was embodied in that Bill ....

MR. BELLOC: For attacks on property.

MR. MACDONALD: My friend's back was turned to me and his voice was thrown so much up that I could not hear his final point, but I understood it elaborated the case of the man who stole a mat. That is all I am clear about. The man who stole the mat did not begin by stealing that mat. As a matter of fact the theory that was contained in that Bill which was described so delightfully by Belloc is a theory which beyond everything is a Collectivist theory. The trouble is that first of all it is said by Belloc that Collectivism is coming un-willingly to the Servile State—and by some of his friends behind—and when I say that this Bill embodied Collectivist theories about punishment he says: "Of course it is, because Collectivism is servility." Well, they cannot have it both ways. But this is only an aside. The fact of the matter is that if Belloc had raised the point earlier and not in the last five minutes, it could be shown that this Bill, as a matter of fact, does embody a very sound idea. It may be abused, undoubtedly, as Socialism can be abused, as everything that applies to our complicated state of society in a general way can be abused, because we are getting further and further away from the time when our legislation can be so precise that a man with some imagination can never caricature it at all and imagine circumstances under which its application would be absolutely absurd. I do not want you to believe for a moment that the picture of the House of Commons, given by Mr. Belloc, is at all a reliable one. Equally unreliable is his statement about what Collectivism is doing. His definition is finally that what we are doing is that we are not providing the proletariat with its own capital, but we are only giving it security. As a matter of fact, the Collectivist idea, and the Collectivist impulse, and the Collectivist demand, which can only be effective when there is a Collectivist majority behind it, is to give the proletariat the capital which is necessary in order to enable it to make a living. It is going to be given in a Collectivist sense, in a co-operative form, but nevertheless, each individual in the community will have his capital and not merely his security. But there was a light that Belloc threw upon his position, which he had not thrown upon it before, by an aside phrase. He seems to assume that if we improve the condition of the people, give them what he calls security, then you are somehow or other reducing the revolutionary capacity. That is altogether wrong. The fact of the matter is that if you keep your people down in slums you are just supplying the instruments for the hands of the vilest form of reaction in this country. Belloc's experience and mine have been rather diverse, even under the same circumstances apparently, but I think it has been the same in this respect. Everyone who has fought a constituency, who has propagated Socialism in the midst of the poorest section of the community, knows that that section is so low down that it has ceased to have any ideals. You can parade your armies of unemployed men in the streets and talk grandiloquently about confiscation and so on, but it amounts to nothing. The thing that you have got to organise is the intelligent, thinking man and woman, who have got the capacity to imagine a better state of things, and if by your Insurance schemes, and by your various other steps that Belloc describes as being mere steps to give more security, you can give men more of the security which means more calmness of mind, which enables them to see clearer the social conditions under which they live, then I say those secure people will be far quicker to come and give us our majority which we want before we can realise the Socialism that Belloc wants to see realised whilst we are in a minority; and so on that fundamental point I join issue with him. We want to make the people more secure and to give them more leisure; we want to give them better goods; we want them to talk less about confiscation, because my experience of the man who does that is, that he is a man who is prepared to confiscate even the possessions of his own comrades and to go over to the other side. My idea of Socialism—and it is the Collectivist idea—is that Socialism is going to come through betterment, not through worsement—that we are going up steadily and uninterruptedly to Socialism, not down and then up with a jump—a most absurd though a very delightful idea.

ONE IN THE AUDIENCE: "What about John Brown?

MR. MACDONALD: The problem of John Brown is still an open problem, and perhaps my friend in the audience will go home quietly and discuss it in the light of more recent enquiries and investigations into the effect of the John Brown rising. However, we will leave that on one side. The final point is Belloc's idea of confiscation. He says: "Why don't you earmark the £19,000,000 taken in Death Duties for the purpose of what he calls confiscating the railways." I thought there was no programme but the programme of confiscation for Belloc. He wants me to go to the House of Commons next week, when railway stock is high, and put down a resolution that the £19,000,000 ought to be set aside for buying out the railways. What would happen? At the end of the week railway stock would be so high that your nineteen millions would not nearly touch it. I will tell you what we will do about railway stock.

MR. BELLOC: This is worth hearing.

MR. MACDONALD: We will continue the process that we have begun and we will depress the exploiting value of railway stock by imposing taxation upon railway incomes, and then when the time suits us and when you are ready we will consider both taxation and purchase, but not one single moment before the time is ready and before the time is ripe, and that is not now.

MR. BELLOC: No, and it never will be.

MR. MACDONALD: It is all very well to say that. We are here on a serious debate. If it is a question of smart reply then we can say to-morrow it will happen, but as serious politicians and as people who want to do something and not merely to talk grandiloquently, you know very well that if the proposition that Belloc advances as a serious contribution to the expenditure of public income and to the nationalisation of railways was taken up by us now it would lead to absolute disaster from both points of view, but that before we are ready for that step to be taken we have to take certain preliminaries, and I can assure you we are doing it. Therefore, again I want to come back to the fundamental position. You have got to criticise Collectivism as a growing concern. You have got to criticise it as a dynamic proposition and not merely as a static one, and it is because Belloc has emphasised it as a static one ....

MR. BELLOC: No.

Mr. MacDonald: And not as a dynamic one that he has first of all confused its present operations with the Servile State, and secondly declined to see that in the change of public opinion and in the new mass of public experience a steadily- growing Collectivism will at last dominate the whole state of society in which we live.

MR. BELLOC: It is my very pleasant duty to move a vote of thanks, as is customary, to the Chair. There is only one original way of doing it, and I have done it myself at least a hundred times, and that is to say that the functions of a Chairman are the most unpleasing of those that anyone can undertake at a great meeting. It is perfectly true. He is quite close to the speakers, he hears the thing in full blast, he is not allowed to say what he thinks, and if there is a row he is concerned. Therefore, I move a vote of thanks to the Chairman.

MR. MACDONALD: I would like to be allowed to second that motion. I hope the Chairman never trembled in his shoes during the whole of the evening, and I hope he will be able to give both Belloc and myself a testimony of good behaviour in spite of the way in which we have been going hammer and tongs at each other.

The resolution was carried by acclamation.

THE CHAIRMAN: I have just to thank you for passing that vote of thanks and to say that I think we have had the most glorious evening; and I hope we shall all be present six months hence to hear the end of this dialectical battle.

The proceedings then terminated.

Made in the USA
Monee, IL
04 November 2026

67375842R00134